Cooking Well

Beautiful Skin

Elizabeth TenHouten

Foreword by David M. Amron, M.D.

"No household should be without this cutting edge publication in its kitchen.... at least no household that places an importance on beautiful skin!"
—David Amron, M.D., Dermatologist

"Everyone should buy this book. The author is a dear friend and is passionate about helping others, and has helped me with many tips for the mature skin!"
—*Denise Vivaldo, chef and owner of Food Fanatics catering company, food stylist, and television producer*

"Elizabeth TenHouten is a beauty/skin care expert, and a huge believer in nature's ability to keep you young—both inside and out."
—*Laurel House, Editor for Discovery Channel's* Planet Green, *and creator of www.greeniq.com*

"Elizabeth is living proof of cooking well for beautiful skin. She has found what works with sincere dedication to wellbeing. Food is not just to satisfy, but to balance and live in harmony with our inner beauty as it radiates, your example is Elizabeth... even more so as she reaches other people with her brilliant recipes."
—*Emily Factor, Emily Factor Designs*

"There are mouth-watering and antioxidant-filled recipes that are easy and delicious. There are so many great ideas from this endearing author that you will want to go the market right after (reading.)"
—Teri Hausman, host of *Beauty Now Radio*

"The latest beauty cookbook on our wish list? *Cooking Well: Beautiful Skin,* by skincare and beauty expert Elizabeth TenHouten. Her delicious and easy-to-follow recipes harness the anti-aging benefits of antioxidants."
—*Kerrie Winick and Andrea Krivelow, creators of celebutantesisters.com*

"Elizabeth is a woman who walks her walk. When you see her, you know she has the credentials to write about beauty for sure!"
—*Tim Martin, founder and CEO of IZO Cleanze (www.izocleanze.com)*

"If you have ever been in the same room with Elizabeth you know that her presence shines and the essence of her being exudes beauty. Her book reveals the taste of beauty. Thank God pomegranate season is upon us, now that I know what a precious delight they are. Pass the `Pretty Poached Salmon,´ please. "
—Karin Inana Solo, Master Healer

Cooking Well: Beautiful Skin
Elizabeth TenHouten
Foreword by David M. Amron, M.D.

Hatherleigh Press is committed to preserving and protecting the natural resources of the Earth. Environmentally responsible and sustainable practices are embraced within the company's mission statement. Hatherleigh Press is a member of the Publishers Earth Alliance, committed to preserving and protecting the natural resources of the planet while developing a sustainable business model for the book publishing industry.

This book was edited and designed in the village of Hobart, New York. Hobart is a community that has embraced books and publishing as a component of its livelihood. There are several unique bookstores in the village. For more information, please visit www.hobartbookvillage.com.

www.hatherleighpress.com

DISCLAIMER
This book offers general cooking and eating suggestions for educational purposes only. In no case should it be a substitute nor replace a healthcare professional. Consult your healthcare professional to determine which foods are safe for you and to establish the right diet for your personal nutritional needs.

Library of Congress Cataloging-in-Publication Data
TenHouten, Elizabeth.
  Cooking well : beautiful skin / Elizabeth TenHouten ; foreword by David Amron.
     p. cm.
  Includes bibliographical references.
  ISBN 978-1-57826-323-3 (pbk. : alk. paper)
  1. Skin--Care and hygiene. 2. Antioxidants--Health aspects. I. Title.
  RL87.T46 2009
  646.7'2--dc22
                          2009039521

Cover Design by Nick Macagnone
Photography by Jon Edwards Photography, Styled by Food Fanatics

hatherleigh
Improve your life. Change your world.

Dedication

For my mother, who taught me the value of inner beauty.
For my husband, who makes me feel beautiful every day.

A Message of Gratitude

I live my life sending out gratitude into the universe, and I would like to thank all those who helped make *Cooking Well: Beautiful Skin* a reality.

I want to especially thank Andrew Flach, Publisher of Hatherleigh Press, for his belief in me and my beauty cookbook. He has a vision for the books he publishes and truly cares that he gives the world healthy ways to live through the written word of his authors. I would also like to extend my sincere gratitude to the rest of my "Hatherleigh Family," for their hard work. A big thanks to Mary Woodward, June Eding, Anna Krusinski, Ryan Tumambing, Nick Macagnone, and all of the awesome people at Hatherleigh Press. I am proud to be your author and friend.

I have a special thank you for my favorite gals, Denise Vivaldo and Cindie Flannigan of Food Fanatics for their belief in me, my recipes, and this book from the very beginning. Denise introduced me to the legendary culinary agency, The Lisa Ekus Group, who signed me, ultimately leading to the publication of this book. I thank Lisa Ekus and Jane Falla for their support and wisdom. Denise is a culinary legend in her own right, and through her honesty and friendship, I always felt encouraged.

I certainly thank my family and friends for their unyielding support and love. I continuously thank my remarkable husband, Christopher Dobson, for his intense love, strength, brilliance, and for making life together fun.

Table of Contents

Foreword

I had the pleasure of meeting Elizabeth TenHouten while hosting my weekly Los Angeles radio show, "The Dr. Amron Hour" with Kerri Kasem. Elizabeth, a featured guest on the show, discussed the importance of cooking with antioxidant-rich ingredients to maintain healthy, nourished skin from the inside out. As I whole heartedly agree with her message, I decided to check out *Cooking Well: Beautiful Skin* for myself.

I was delighted to scour through this unique beauty cookbook. In addition to the 75 user-friendly (even I could execute them!) and tasty recipes she features, Elizabeth TenHouten also includes 50 creative antioxidant Beauty Bytes—simple, fun tips for achieving beautiful skin. Even with my extremely busy schedule, I experimented with preparing many of the delicious antioxidant-rich recipes in this book. The main ingredients in each dish are, of course, rich in antioxidant and therefore possess high nutritional values. My personal favorite of these is the Rainbow Salad. I highly suggest trying it for yourself!

The most unique aspect of *Cooking Well: Beautiful Skin*, in my opinion, is Elizabeth TenHouten's underlying message of the importance in discovering one's authentic inner beauty. Even though I am a cosmetic surgeon, I realize that beauty is more than just skin deep and inner beauty can be far more alluring and powerful than outer beauty. In my practice, I do many nonsurgical procedures to rejuvenate the face and combat the effects of aging and the environment. I therefore have a close understanding of the contribution of a proper diet in achieving radiant skin.

I was happy to discover that this beauty cookbook relays this truth and encourages readers to embrace their inner beauty. Our bodies are miraculous organisms and it is so critical that we care for ourselves in body and soul.

Cooking Well: Beautiful Skin has my professional endorsement as I find it to be a complete guide for achieving healthy and beautiful skin through simple diet and lifestyle changes. Elizabeth TenHouten is a creative and eloquent author who has much knowledge to impart to her readers. No household should be without this cutting-edge publication in its kitchen… at least no household that places an importance on beautiful skin!

David M. Amron, M.D. is a Beverly Hills-based, board-certified dermatologic and cosmetic surgeon specializing in liposuction surgery and cosmetic dermatology. He is a fellow of the American Academy of Cosmetic Surgery, American Society for Dermatologic Surgery, American Society for Liposuction Surgery, and the American Society for Laser Medicine and Surgery. Dr. Amron has published numerous articles in the medical literature and lectures nationally. His expert work has been featured on CNN, BBC, the Discovery Channel, *People* magazine and numerous other media publications.

Dubbed "The Liposuction Guru to the Stars" by Entertainment Tonight, Dr. Amron has meticulously sculpted thousands of patients from around the world in his 15 years of practice and is highly respected for achieving consistently outstanding results with pure local anesthesia. He is also a specialist in revision liposuction surgery and is renowned for improving and perfecting the work of other surgeons.

Dr. Amron has a vast knowledge of cosmetic dermatology. He specializes in anti-aging and facial rejuvenation treatments through non-surgical procedures such as lasers, botox, and fillers with exceptional success and optimum cosmetic elegance. Through his comprehensive approach to the aging face, Dr. Amron has beautified innumerable patients who have come to know and trust him with all of their skin care needs

Introduction

Cooking Well: Beautiful Skin defines beauty as one's authentic, inner self. The existential concept that we are always in a state of becoming, suggests that our inner self is always growing, never stagnant. Through one's self-awareness and connection with the true beauty within oneself, the cultivation of inner beauty grows richer. This gives us the opportunity to improve ourselves and become our most beautiful actualized self.

At the heart of this book is the understanding of the value of attaining beauty through the balance of body and soul. In fully nourishing such a balance, this book will not only offer antioxidant-rich recipes to help you achieve a beautiful complexion, but will also show you how to obtain a complete love of your authentic, beautiful self through meditation exercises, inspirational quotes and poems. You will also gain valuable insight into how you can discover the inherent beauty of self-love, inspiring you to become your most beautiful self, inside and out.

In an effort to treat skin internally and nourish one's self from the inside, *Cooking Well: Beautiful Skin* addresses all skin-types as a whole, without categorizing a typology of skin. Indulge in skin beautifying and educative "Beauty Bytes," secrets for beautiful skin. Your skin will glow with a radiant complexion when you eat the antioxidant-rich meals found in this book. The very act of taking care of yourself and striving for healthy, beautiful skin, is an act of self-love. Cooking with antioxidant-rich ingredients is the healthy, beautiful way to nourish your body, in its totality.

"When we speak of Nature it is wrong to forget that we are ourselves a part of Nature. We ought to view ourselves with the same curiosity and openness with which we study a tree, the sky or a thought, because we too are linked to the entire universe."

—Henry Matisse

Chapter 1

Antioxidants and Beauty

Antioxidants and Your Skin

Antioxidants are responsible for preventing free radicals from oxidizing, thus slowing the aging process and preventing disease. The human body is not capable of producing antioxidants. Therefore, in order to prevent the oxidant process and protect ourselves against the skin damage from exposure to free radicals, we must incorporate antioxidant foods into our diet.

Free radicals are highly reactive chemicals that attack molecules by capturing electrons and modifying their chemical structures. One of the harmful effects of these toxic molecules is gene mutation, which affects the ability of the skin to repair itself, causing aging. Biologically speaking, antioxidants donate electrons to stabilize and, in effect, neutralize the harmful effects of free radicals. Ultraviolet radiation (sun exposure) and airborne pollutants such as cigarette smoke, both commonly found in the environment, are examples of free radicals. Smokers often find the glow in their skin restored once they quit. Essentially, antioxidants cancel the cell-damaging effects of free radicals and help restore your skin to its natural state.

"We are a part of nature as a whole, whose order we follow."
—Spinoza

1

Free radical damage is closely associated with oxidation damage, because free radicals are released as a result of oxidation. This is the process that occurs when oxygen molecules interact with different substances. Some common examples are the rusting of iron, the browning of sliced apples, and the aging of your skin. For humans, the process of oxidation is commonly linked with the breakdown of collagen in one's skin, which causes wrinkling and aging. Furthermore, oxidation works to continuously burn calories to produce energy for our cells, so that we can function and live. However, this process of oxidation, while enabling us to live, releases free radicals, making the consumption of antioxidants essential for promoting health and glowing skin.

Antioxidants to the Rescue

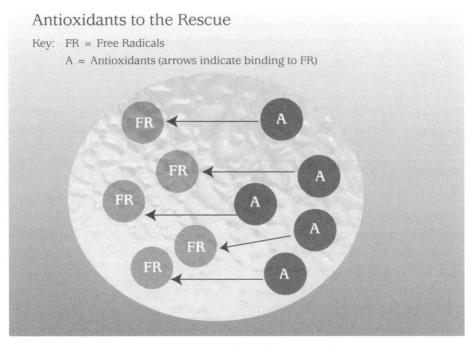

Key:　FR = Free Radicals
　　　A = Antioxidants (arrows indicate binding to FR)

The human body can't produce its own natural antioxidants, leaving us to rely solely upon our diet to nourish our body and to maintain beautiful skin, and prevent aging. Fruits and vegetables are an excellent source of natural antioxidants, which is why they are common ingredients in the recipes in this book. Furthermore, this book offers plenty of creative recipes for appetizers, entrées, desserts, and snacks, to help you incorporate antioxidants into any meal of the day.

The beauty attained by cooking with antioxidant-rich foods does not stop in the

"There is a kind of beauty in imperfection."
—Conrad Hall

2

kitchen. Beauty is a multifaceted splendor—the more beautiful you feel within and the more you care about yourself, the more beautiful you will be on the outside. To help you achieve your truest, most authentic beauty, I have also included antioxidant-rich beauty recipes and "Beauty Bytes" to accompany the many delicious meals you'll find in this book.

Outer and Inner Beauty

Our outer beauty and aesthetics reflect an inner beauty, well-being, and sense of self. The warmth and contentment shown in a smile, or the love shown in the twinkle of our lover's eyes, draws us to the face. If one's eyes are truly the windows to the souls, then our face is our mirror of one's self to the world. It reveals our favorable tastes, distastes, curiosities, longings, passions, doubts, sympathies, loves, and desires. Our faces, our complexions, are reflections of our souls.

Nurture Your Inner Beauty

Inside each of us there is a beauty waiting to be touched, to be awakened by our love for ourselves. Self-love radiates from within us as a glow. It is important to stay in tune with yourself and to nurture your inner beauty. Every morning, as you arise from your slumber, close your eyes and smile. You are smiling to yourself—what a beautiful way to arise and wake up your beauty! Take the time to think positive, beautiful, peaceful thoughts. These can be thoughts of inspiration or something specific that is important to you. Either way, be sure to make yourself a priority and take time out for yourself (even if it is just a brief moment as you are waking up), before you think or do anything else.

"Integrity reveals beauty."
—Thomas Leonard

"Beauty of whatever kind, in its supreme development, invariably excites the sensitive soul to tears."
—Edgar Alan Poe

"Inner beauty should be the most important part of improving one's self."
—Priscilla Presley

"Personal beauty is a greater recommendation than any letter of reference."
—Aristotle

"Let us live for the beauty of
our own reality."
—Charles Lamb

Chapter 2

Awaken Your Inner Beauty

Loving Thoughts

The following are some loving, inspirational thoughts that I have created for myself, and I share them with you in the hope that you may accept them into your own thoughts each morning. These loving thoughts can be read aloud or silently to yourself and can also be used as ideas for a journal exercise.

"If we are not beautiful to each other, we cannot know beauty in any form."
—Dorothy Allison

I recommend that you engage yourself in a journal exercise as an opportunity to connect with yourself. Relax in a comfy chair with a soft pillow underneath your head. Open your journal to a blank page, and envision this page as your template for a deeper realization of who you are and what you long for. Write down one of the loving thoughts below or create your own. Once you have written down a loving thought, read it and re-read it. Allow yourself to find truth in those words and their relationship to who you are and who you are becoming. Taking the time each morning to think these pleasant, healing thoughts will help you reduce stress, which is yet another cause of skin imperfections. So, de-stress your mind and clear your skin.

> "If either man or woman would realize that the full power of personal beauty, it must be by cherishing noble thoughts and hopes and purposes; by having something to do and something to live for that is worthy of humanity, and which, by expanding and symmetry to the body which contains it."
> —Rose Kennedy

> "Being is desirable because it is identical with beauty, and beauty is loved because it is being. We ourselves possess beauty when we are true to our own being; ugliness is in going over to another order; knowing ourselves, we are beautiful; in self-ignorance, we are ugly."
> —Ambrose Bierce

Loving Thought I: Overcoming Obstacles

There is no hardship so great inside myself that I may not triumph with self-love.

Finding strength inside yourself to deal with the hardships in your life is a healing exercise. You will find that if you love yourself, you can overcome anything and each time you overcome an obstacle you will continue to become enlightened. Say this thought to yourself, or out loud to proclaim your strength to carry on. As creation arises from destruction, so will new life and new beauty arise from hardships you overcome. Create your beauty, inside and out, beginning with this loving thought.

Loving Thought II: Mutuality

It is my nature to love myself and to love others who know not yet their wonders.

You, like all human beings, are born with the innate desire and need to love not only yourself, but to love others as well. According to Abraham Maslow's theory on the hierarchy of needs, the need to love and the need to be loved are among our most basic, fundamental human needs. Looking at how this affects your everyday life, it is simple to recognize that you need love from yourself as well as love from others. You can do a good deed by extending love to your fellow human being. This love may eventually come back to you, continuing the infinite, loving, energetic flow of life from which grows your beautiful thoughts.

Loving Thought III: Wholeness

The essence of my beauty is known to only those who know my mind and my soul.

I cannot emphasize enough the deep-rooted connection between our inner beauty and our outer beauty. If you show the world your beautiful mind and your beautiful soul, I promise you, the world will look at you and see beauty.

Loving Thought IV: Authenticity

I am a unique being, radiating my inner, authentic self as beauty.

You are as original and precious as every snowflake that has ever fallen from the sky. By being your authentic self you can become more beautiful than you ever thought possible. So, dare to be you! Dare to be a true, unique, genuine, beautiful you.

Loving Thought V: Growth

I have the gift of self-love, so my being shines brightly, inside and out.

Inner beauty stems from self-love. We all have inner beauty. As a seed is watered to bloom into a beautiful flower, when our inner beauty is nourished with self-love, we grow to become our best self. I challenge you to visualize yourself as the flower that has already blossomed. This visualization is the first step to becoming beautiful inside and out.

Loving Thought VI: Opportunity

Chances for beauty await me today, so I will nourish myself, and cook for beauty.

Cooking Well: Beautiful Skin is simply another way to nourish your seed of inner beauty. Take advantage of every chance you have to cook antioxidant-rich recipes for your skin. The glow and beauty of your skin is evidence of true inner and outer beauty.

"Beauty is in the heart of the beholder."
—H. G. Wells

"The future belongs to those who believe in the beauty of their dreams."
—Eleanor Roosevelt

"Through loyalty to the past, our mind refuses to realize that tomorrow's joy is possible only if today's makes way for it; that each wave owes the beauty of its line only to the withdrawal of the preceding one."
—Andre Gide

"The pain passes, but the beauty remains."
—Pierre Auguste Renoir

7

"*As we grow old,
the beauty steals inward.*"
—Ralph Waldo Emerson

Chapter 3

Age and Beautiful Skin

Aging Gracefully

Aging gracefully stems from the way you nourish yourself and your body. Our complexion, our face, is the most telling revealer of age. By cooking with antioxidant-rich ingredients you are caring for your skin and allowing your face to reveal the youth that lies within, despite your chronological age.

A dull complexion can be an honest reflection into a dull or uninspired spirit. However, a youthful glow, a spark in one's eyes, or a carefree, welcoming smile can be an honest glance into the soul of an inspired, caring person who takes care of herself. Joy is written all over her face, and she is beautiful. Each and every one of us can achieve the beauty that lies in glowing, youthful skin. Care for yourself and seek the highest potential of your own inner and outer beauty, and you will begin to notice your inner youthfulness shining through.

"For age is opportunity no less
Than youth itself
Though in another dress,
And as the evening twilight
fades away
The sky is filled with stars
invisible by day."
—Henry Wadsworth Longfellow

Chapter 4

Balanced Skin

Harmony of Body, Harmony of Mind

In nature and in life, things that exist harmoniously are able to flourish and prosper to their fullest potential. Humans living in harmony with one another have a more peaceful sense of balance and feel supported by positive energy, and thus are able to achieve greatness. Harmony is a beautiful gift that we should strive for.

> "The ideas that have lighted my way have been kindness, beauty and truth."
> —Albert Einstein

Harmony is important in all aspects of living, including our physical body. Even the regulation of temperature in the body must be harmonious and appropriately balanced in order to feel comfortable in our own skin. Imagine if your upper body was comfortable and warm, while your lower body was freezing cold. This ill-balanced body temperature would likely make you feel uncomfortable, and might even make you feel pain in your own skin.

To live in a state of disharmony is painful on physical, emotional, and psychological levels. You must take complete care of your whole body, inside and out. You might take proper blood flow and circulation for granted, but like every other incredible bodily function you have, they must be nurtured.

Unbalanced bodily functions may also negatively affect your mind. Your carefree thoughts, and even your intensely focused thoughts, would be shoved aside while your mind copes with the lack of harmony within your body. Beauty in all things—including bodily features and peace of mind—is rooted in the fundamental principles of nature in balance.

Your mind is an incredibly powerful and creative aspect of who you are. Capable of defining who you are to yourself, your mind is a sanctuary of self-worth, self-love, self-knowledge, and self-identity.

Just as your body must be in harmony with itself, so must your mind. Imagine if your thoughts were not harmonious with one another. I am not talking about the mind's ability to consider the values of different opinions, or the mind's ability to rationally discriminate between two varying, but equally logical possibilities. I am talking about a thought you believe to be true. Certainly you can change your mind with more knowledge or experience, but you cannot maintain a thought that you believe to be true while simultaneously holding the negation of this thought to also be true. The thought can be as simple as, "the sounds of a violin are beautifully soothing to my soul" versus "the sounds of a violin are disturbing and give me a headache." A balanced mind is unable to accept both of these thoughts as simultaneous truths.

There are many varying degrees of this imbalance or disharmony of the mind. Many of us may live in less intense conflict of thought, and remain imbalanced at other, less obvious, levels. In some cases, these less obvious forms of imbalance can be as damaging to self-healing as a severely imbalanced state of being. A return to nature is all about finding your sense of peace and a balance between mind and body.

Harmony and balance are at the core of the connection between mind and body, which translates as "beauty" in the diagram on page 13. There is a syncing of energetic waves through our body and our mind.

Love   Health

Self-Knowledge

Nourishment

Thoughts   *Balance*

Mind Beauty Body

Harmony

Skin

Self-worth

Dreams

Recognizing that the energies of our mind and body are connected can give you the strength and focus to achieve a balance and sense of wellness.

Antioxidants are a component of this connection because our body, our skin, needs nourishment for a healthy balance. In addition, as we nourish our skin with antioxidant-rich recipes, we are feeding our brains, as well!

"Rare is the union of beauty and purity."
—Juvenal

There are many components through which we can channel our energy. For instance, our dreams and hopes for the future must be in harmony and balance with our health. Without optimal health, our future dreams may not be realized. Another important focus of energetic flow is through self-knowledge. Episteme, or knowledge, has a greater depth than simply "knowing information". There are many types of knowledge including, but not limited to: experiential knowledge, or what we come to know through our life experience, is a knowledge of each of our personal journeys. Innate knowledge is what we know by virtue of our own minds, through reason, apart from experience. Self-knowledge is a combination of both experiential knowledge and innate knowledge, as we are beings of our environment and

"Beauty itself is but the sensible image of the Infinite."

—Sir Francis Bacon

our genetic abilities for rationality. The more we think about ourselves in relation to our life experiences, the higher our self-knowledge will be. Self-knowledge is simply a knowing of one's self. It is through knowledge of the self that we can best nourish the self.

All of these components are interrelated and intertwined to create a harmonious flow of energy to obtain beauty. There is an infinite living connection and flow between your mind and your body. The nourishment and functioning of your body's organs is based on what you decide to put into your body. If you drink water and cook for beauty, your body will be nourished properly and function beautifully. Beauty lies within how you nourish your mind and how you nourish your body. It is as simple as that!

"Nature does nothing uselessly."
—Aristotle

Chapter 5

Hydration for Beauty

Drink Your Skin Beautiful

Hydration is the key to a supple, clear, dewy complexion. The beverage of your skin's choice is water. Nourish your skin, the largest organ in your body, with moisturizing creams and moisturizing cleansers. We do not want to eliminate the natural and essential oils in the skin, but rather achieve a balance.

Water constitutes 90 percent of your blood, 75 percent of your brain and muscles, 25 percent of your body fat, and 22 percent of your bone. Water is a life source. During life, your body is approximately 70 percent water. At birth this percentage is around 90 percent, while at life's end it is closer to 50 percent. This gradual decrease in your body's water content is yet another reason why it is so important to continuously rehydrate by drinking plenty of water. After all, we need water just as we need oxygen! Including water, women should drink nine cups of liquid daily and men thirteen cups of liquid daily. Despite the wide variety of liquid drinks that can help to hydrate you, I recommend relying solely on water as your liquid source for keeping your skin hydrated.

"upon
soft skin shimmer
red petals, dew drops dance
after cool summer shower, kiss
silk skin"
—Gregg Rowe,
"Soft Skin Petals"

Become a Water Connoisseur

You can train your palate to become a water connoisseur. At first taste, close your eyes and try to notice the weight of the gulp on your tongue. Notice how it rushes to fill your mouth, above and beneath your tongue. Feel the temperature of the water completely adjust to match the temperature inside your mouth. Now, pay attention to the sudden weightlessness of the water. Notice how your body actually pulls the water down your throat as if with each swallow, it is showing its gratitude to you for nourishing yourself. Nourish yourself and love yourself.

Bottled Water: Finding a Favorite

There are many different brands of bottled water on the market today. Most grocery stores have an entire aisle dedicated to bottled water. Each brand has subtle distinctions in taste, and your choice is a completely personal preference.

I recommend that you do a taste test of several different brands of water in order to discover your preference. I personally love Brita filtered water because, aside from its fresh taste, I always have chilled water available to drink.

Drinking bottled water on a regular basis can become very expensive, not to mention the impact all those plastic bottles have on the environment. As a more economical and environmentally friendly alternative, use filtered tap water instead. If your refrigerator is fitted with a water dispenser, the water from that is already filtered and is always cold—just remember to change your filter as often as the manufacturer requires. Usually, there is a light inside the refrigerator that illuminates when the filter needs to be replaced.

For those who do not have a refrigerator that dispenses water, you are in luck: Brita, a pitcherlike container with a filter that you fill with tap water, quickly filters the water and transforms your unfiltered tap water into pristine drinking water. For more information about Brita's water filtering system, check out their informative website at: www.brita.com.

There are creative ways to drink all the water your body requires daily. Make it fun for yourself! Throw some delicious raspberries or sliced strawberries into your glass or bottle of water. A challenge is born: now, you must finish the water to reach the berries. Hydrated skin appears supple, smooth, and glowing, so love your water, no matter what the source.

"Water is fluid, soft and yielding. But water will wear away rock, which is rigid and cannot yield. As a rule, whatever is fluid, soft, and yielding will overcome whatever is rigid and hard. This is another paradox: what is soft is strong."
—Lao-Tzu (600 B.C.)

Dehydration Knows No Beauty

Dehydration is revealed most obviously through peeling or cracked lips and flaking cheeks, nose, chin, and forehead. In some cases dehydrated skin can lose its natural, healthy color, too. Flaky, dry skin can be itchy, and scratching only causes inflammatory redness.

Sun damage appears as uneven color tone, areas of discoloration or "sun spots" (also called "age spots"), and of course sunburn. The sun literally cooks your skin, robbing it of essential oils and dehydrating it. Use sunscreen!

Once you have cleansed and moisturized the surface of your skin, sunscreen is the most critical product you will put on your beautiful, clean face. Sunscreen acts both as a preventative measure against the damaging effects of the sun (dryness, dehydration, discoloration) and as a moisturizer, softening your skin. There are sunscreens with various sun protection factor (SPF). The higher the number, the better protected you will be from the sun's damaging rays. Try an SPF value of thirty or higher. Most facial moisturizing products do contain some amount of SPF. Just do not neglect your neck and chest.

Drier skin shows the earliest signs of aging as fine lines and wrinkles. This is not what we want. If we are to obtain glowing, supple, healthy skin, water has to become your beverage of choice. Water helps the body to function properly, particularly in the liver, which works to filter toxins, helping maintain a balanced skin health. Water also helps to achieve a pH balance of the skin. Unbalanced pH levels can result in oily, eel-like skin.

"Beauty is the gift of God."
—Aristotle

Chapter 6

Sleep, Rest, and Meditation for Your Complexion

Sleepy? Well, Rest!

Sleeping Beauty ought to be the spokesperson for a radiant complexion. Her prince found her glowing, rested complexion irresistible. Rest is pivotal for feeling well and looking our best. Not having adequate sleep really shows in your skin.

> "I slept and dreamed that life was beauty."
> —Ellen Stugis Hooper

You do not necessarily need to sleep extra hours in order to feel well-rested. There are other methods, in addition to sleep, that are helpful in revealing your beauty. Deep, intentional inhalations followed by soothing, thorough exhalations cleanse your lungs of stale air, and deliver more oxygen to your brain, allowing you to concentrate at a superior level.

There are several techniques for becoming a more rested person in general. There are breathing exercises that can help you feel more rested and balanced, such as Hatha yoga, which focuses on breathing, and is very relaxing.

Meditation and Soothing Your Inner Self

Resting or meditation is calming and stress alleviating, which improves the visible quality of our inner being, giving our skin a radiant complexion.

> "If your meditation
> Is truly high and deep,
> Then you are bound to have
> A silent dialogue with
> peace."
> —Sri Chinmoy

> "Returning to the deepest
> truth of our being can bring
> us back to ourselves."
> —Heidegger

Meditation is important for finding your center, and allowing yourself to focus on taking slow, relaxed, and controlled breaths. Our center is where we recognize our true selves and gain a sense of appreciation for who we are.

Focusing on breathing is the foundation for accessing the meditative state of being. Breath connects us intimately with the world around us.

Meditation Exercises

The following meditation exercises are meant to still your mind, calm your soul, and create balance and harmony for your beautiful self. Embrace this opportunity to experience your beautiful self without judgment or pressure. Just feel yourself— melt into yourself.

Breathing Meditation Exercise

Slowly breathe in and out, paying attention to the rising and falling of the breath as it moves rhythmically through your lungs. Notice that your whole body responds to your inhale and exhale.

Inhale deeply through your nose, completely filling your lungs, and hold the air captive inside yourself for four seconds. Exhale thoroughly with your whole body and mind. Allow the thoughts that fill your mind to escape with the air. Release yourself from your mental images and ideas. Hold your breath for another four seconds before you engage your lungs in another inhale. Repeat this inhaling and exhaling, holding for four seconds between each breath. After five inhales and five exhales you may return to your normal breathing pattern.

As your mind starts to wander into a stream of consciousness, collect yourself and return to focusing on your breathing. Soon, you will become focused inward, feeling unaware of your surroundings and tuned out to everything but the essential beauty of your self. Stay there and experience yourself. You are a being of beauty.

Listening Meditation Exercise

Let us connect with silence and be open to the sounds of our inner souls. Listen to what your heart longs for. Listen to what your spirit is inspired by. Listen to what awakens your very core being. I want you to hear yourself and nothing else.

Connect with the silence and let it gradually, and ever so gently, keep you centered inward. Listen with your heart and your authentic inner self. You will eventually hear nothing.

White Rose Meditation Exercise

Our center is where we connect with the essence of our authentic being. This sense of self translates into a beaming aura from within, reflected outwards by a glowing face. This is the very definition of beauty. To know one's self is a great gift and, like beauty, it shines from within. The goal of meditation is to know one's self, something often referred to as illumination.

Close your eyes and breathe with ease and purpose. Connect with your authentic beautiful self. Grant yourself permission to be revealed in your true form—a beautiful being. Once you have welcomed this experience, picture the tightly closed bud of a white rose with a shiny emerald stem. Imagine that your truth, your self, blooms with the slow, meaningful opening of the rose's petals, one by one. Your inner world has its own reality, its own essence. This is the quidditas, or essence, of who you are existentially becoming.

Exist in this process with yourself. Learn more of who you are with the blossoming of each soft petal from your white rose. Let each petal represent a part of you, whether

"Stop the words now. Open the window in the center of your chest, And let spirit fly in and out."
—Mevlana Rumi

"Flowers... are a proud assertion that a ray of beauty outvalues all the utilities of the world."
—Ralph Waldo Emerson

"Know Thyself."
—Aristotle

"Enhance and intensify one's vision of that synthesis of truth and beauty which is the highest and deepest reality."
—Ovid

> "You are just like a rose, a lesson of beauty, to whom a memory, but forever remembered."
> —A. Neilen

> "To love beauty is to see light."
> —Victor Hugo

it is your thoughts, your hopes, your fears, or your anxieties. Whatever is part of you, I want you to connect with it and understand that it deserves your attention. You are worthy of your own undivided attention. Meet these feelings, or petals, without judgment. Suspending judgment of others allows you to come to a greater understanding of their core person, their character. You are entitled to the same suspension of judgment. Accept yourself and your grand, boundless beauty.

With the visualized opening and blooming of each separate rose petal, recognize a part of yourself; meet it in truth and with acceptance. If you love yourself and the essential you, your white rose will never wilt. Feel what is inside your heart. What do you long for? Do you want to live happily, or long to be healthy? Quietly repeat your wishes to yourself over and over until you are present only to your longing for yourself. You should feel as though your thoughts are synchronized with the present moment and with your longing. It is a simultaneity—or coming together—of what is now, and what you wish for. You are essentially in your own loving world, where the only meaning applied to anything is your sincere longing and your desire to connect with yourself.

Golden Beauty Light Meditation Exercise

Once more, as you prepare to engage yourself in a meditative state, you will begin in a comfortable position, breathing in and out deeply.

As you arrive at a state of calm and you are able to receive yourself, imagine a pure golden light moving completely through your body and extending out of the top of your head. Visualize that this intense golden light touches your physical body, your organs, your cells, and your spiritual body. You are beautiful and this light illuminates that beauty. Notice and feel your spirit's connection to the golden light of beauty. Allow the calm to overtake your being. Surrender to the serenity as it fills your being.

Spoken Meditation Exercise

This spoken meditation exercise is a method of communicating with your subconscious and connecting with your true self. The totality of the self cannot be grasped in its entirety because we are always in a state of becoming. To connect with yourself is essentially being present to your state of becoming. Through deep meditation you can focus inward towards the essence of your self. By identifying yourself with your secrets and inner truths, you will set yourself free.

We have defined beauty as your authentic, inner self. With this in mind, focus on your authentic self, your beauty, and all that you are, all that you desire, all of your secrets, everything that makes you who you are and who you are becoming. Repeat to yourself the word "beauty" over and over again in your mind. With each natural exhale, say this word to yourself and focus on the meaning of it and the love it brings. You are creating a sanctuary in your heart to open yourself to the presence of love. Connect with your self. You are beautiful.

The goal of meditation is to go beyond the mind. One cannot achieve a meditative state of mind with thought. Silence your mind, escape your thoughts and simply be. Be and become your beautiful, authentic inner self.

Meditation Prayer
I ask all blessings,
I ask them with reverence,
Of my mother the Earth,
Of the sky, moon, and sun my father.
I am old age: The essence of life,
I am the source of all happiness.
All is peaceful, all in beauty,
All in harmony, all in joy.
—Navaho Anonymous

Chapter 7

Makeup and Your Skin

Chloe's Skin

When I worked as a makeup artist, I had a client whom I will call 'Chloe' who suffered from extraordinarily dry skin. Though she appeared to be in her mid- to late-twenties, possibly even younger, her dry skin had aged her, and robbed her of her natural glow. Chloe initially came to my makeup counter, intending to find a foundation that would match her coloring and also moisturize her skin. I was confident I could find her a foundation; I was a color analyst and had learned how to analyze the skin's undertone versus the overtone, so I could then match a foundation to suit the client's true skin tone.

Once I found a foundation that blended perfectly with her skin tone, I first applied a generous amount of dry-skin moisturizer to her face. Moments later, I applied the foundation to her face, using a synthetic fiber foundation brush, which is engineered to make blending more efficient. However, Chloe and I were not pleased with the foundation's appearance on her skin. The foundation color was indeed an exact match, but it did not blend into her skin. There was clearly a problem with her skin that was not being corrected, even with an intense moisturizer, silky foundation, and a superior blending foundation brush.

Chloe shared with me her frustrations with her taut, dry skin. She also told me that she applied a heavy, creamy moisturizer twice daily, to no avail.

"When the soul looks out of its body, it should see only beauty in its path. These are the sights we must hold in mind, in order to move to a higher place."

—Yusef Lateef

Chloe came to me with the hope that I had the perfect products to help make her skin look beautifully smooth and soft to the touch. Quite honestly, this is never the case.

I can attest to the fact that I have never seen anyone's skin improve from having beautifully applied makeup, if their skin was not originally in excellent condition. Nor have I ever seen anyone with beautiful skin look better with beautifully applied makeup, if they do not radiate a glow from their inner beauty.

In this sense, it does matter what you bring to the counter. Your skin is the clearest indicator of the results you are likely to obtain at a cosmetic counter. Caring for your skin in your own precious time is the only way to leave satisfied after a visit to the department store makeup counter. You are in control of your skin, your body, and your mind. This is an empowering piece of information and inspiration for you. You can help make yourself look beautiful by following my philosophy of *Cooking Well: Beautiful Skin*.

"There is so much beauty in life,
Beauty in the human soul,
Beauty in the heart and in the mind
Of the good man and woman.
There is beauty in nature,
Beauty in the sky and in the clouds,
In the mountains and in the sea.
There is beauty in the creative work of man.
Beauty in true friendship.
And immeasurable beauty in love.
All God's blessing
To delight us in this world."

—Emily Nielsen Reyes de Gaspar, Reflections

Chapter 8

Healthy Skin Is Beautiful

Skin Health

Having healthy skin promotes the health of your body. As I mentioned in Chapter 5, one of the functions of your liver is to filter toxins. But the burden of filtering toxins does not rest upon your liver alone. An incredible amount of our body's toxins are actually filtered through the skin!

The billions of pores in our skin release toxins through sweat. Some areas of our skin produce more sweat than others. For instance, our underarms release a much greater amount of toxins on a daily basis than the skin that makes up our eyelids.

By sweating, healthy skin undergoes an acidic reaction as it expels toxins through its pores. For this reason, skin is often referenced as the third kidney. This is why drinking water is so vital to maintaining beautiful skin. The more water you drink, the more "watered-down" the toxins in your body will become, and the more toxins you will be able to release through your skin and other organs, namely the liver. It's a fact—your beauty is contingent upon your mental, emotional and physical health.

Exercise for Your Skin

Since your skin's pores release toxins when you sweat, break a sweat for beauty's sake! Exercise in whatever form you prefer: intense cardio, peaceful yoga, thoughtful meditation, Pilates, lifting weights—just make sure you break a sweat. You may be less likely to break a sweat during thoughtful meditation, which exercises your mind, than if you were running on a treadmill. That said, I recommend doing a combination of high-impact and low-impact exercises, ensuring that you will sweat and help your body to filter toxins through your skin at its optimum capacity.

Besides your body feeling better after releasing all those poisonous toxins through your skin, you will feel more emotionally balanced as well. Exercise is a builder of self-esteem and self-love. While many people believe that they need someone else to motivate them to commit to exercising, I really believe that your own beauty is all the motivation you need. So, let yourself and your beauty be your motivating factor to start an exercise routine. Take control of your own health and beauty, for they are one and the same. Rejoice in this responsibility and motivate yourself with your tempting potential for beauty.

Cleanse Your Skin

Your dewy, glowing complexion can be the result of the internal cleansing that water, combined with antioxidant recipes, naturally gives you. Nevertheless, external cleansing is also important. Moisturizers, facial toners, and facial soaps play a critical role as the support system for the internal nourishment you are providing your skin by following the principles in this book.

"It is time for parents to teach young people early on that in diversity there is beauty and there is strength."
—Maya Angelou

Chapter 9

Cultural Ideas of Beauty and Skincare

Cultures around the world revere beauty. The Greeks prayed to Aphrodite, the goddess of beauty. She was the most desired of all the goddesses, a symbol of the reverence for beauty. Beauty, in whatever form it is recognized, is valued and sought after across the globe.

On an island off the coast of Indonesian Sumatra, Mentawai women file each of their teeth to a sharp point. Tooth filing is a beautification practice among the Mentawai women. The process is done without anesthetic and can be quite painful. But the Mentawai feel that the pain is a small price to pay for the beauty they attain from a sharpened smile. You can truly see this Mentawai woman smiling from her heart. She is simply beautiful.

Beauty is in the eye of the beholder; whether represented by sharp teeth or a straight smile. What is most significant

"In every man's heart there is a secret nerve that answers to the vibrations of beauty."
—Christopher Morely

Source: Royle, David. 2003. Body Perfect. http://www.nationalgeographic.com/series/taboo/1851/overview [2003].

"Beauty is no quality in things themselves: It exists merely in the mind which contemplates them; and each mind perceives a different beauty."

—David Hume

about these seemingly disparate views of beauty is that, beyond specifics such as the shape of someone's smile, the ultimate definition of beauty is communicated through complexion. Soft, supple skin is universally valued as a sign of youth and beheld as a marker of beauty in all cultures.

Your complexion remains an honest conveyer of your beauty, serving as a bridge between others' eyes and your spirit within. Your complexion is an incredibly important part of sharing your beauty with all who see you. Achieving an inner and outer beauty will be shown in your glowing complexion, which is only attained by one who indeed knows who they are.

Ancient cultures have created different methods of skincare. Beauty was an important part of life in ancient Egypt, for example. Egyptians used vegetable oils to smooth their skin in the heat. Both men and women indulged in this beautifying skin treatment, and even wore particular scents as part of their culture's standard of beauty. Particularly, they used almond oil for aromatherapy and holistic purposes. "For the ancient Egyptians, beauty, magic, and medicine were inseparable." Sensual eye makeup, as worn by Cleopatra, was just as popular then as it is today. The Egyptians made eye-liner from mesdemet, which is derived from galena, a mineral known to have disinfectant qualities in addition to its attractive hue as an eye-liner. Beauty and health are synonymous, and the Egyptian beauty treatments are a perfect example of this.

The Brazilians ate the jojoba bean, as well as seaweed, a powerful antioxidant, to maintain a beautiful complexion. For centuries, Asian cultures have also relied upon the jojoba bean, as well as seaweed, a powerful antioxidant, to achieve glowing skin. The Chinese actually look at the skin as a way of determining the health of the whole body. Our skin is, after all, our body's largest organ.

As one universe, and one energy, all ethnicities and cultures seek beauty. The nature of beauty is that it does not take one particular form but reaches us universally. For beauty is inside each of us.

Goddesses of Beauty

In every culture, goddesses have always been beautiful, or at least represented an idealized version of beauty.

The Maori people of New Zealand worship the Hineahuone, also known as the First Woman. As explained in Hana Weka's Maori story, Hineahuone was made from her mother, the Earth. Two of Earth's sons adorned their mother with great beauty, dressing her "in a beautiful gown that shimmered green and gold in the sunlight." They created Hineahuone, or First Woman, so that Earth's new beauty might be enjoyed.

The Greeks worshiped Aphrodite, the goddess of beauty. For the Irish and Scottish cultures, Clionda is the goddess of beauty. The Hindu culture valued Lakshmi as the goddess of abundance and beauty. Beauty in all cultures is valued, and even worshiped in the form of goddesses.

"The night is beautiful,
So the faces of my people.
The stars are beautiful,
So the eyes of my people.
Beautiful, also, is the sun.
Beautiful, also are the souls
of my people."
–Langston Hughes, My People

"*Love of beauty is taste.*
The creation of beauty is art."
—Ralph Waldo Emerson

Chapter 10

Antioxidant-Rich Recipes

My philosophy of caring for one's skin by cooking recipes infused with antioxidant-rich ingredients is rooted in the philosophy of loving one's self. Beauty, as we have established, is expressed internally and externally. When we look at the totality of our selves, we are more than anatomy, more than skin, so let us not forget the value of our spirit. Once we grasp the composition of the body and mind, we are free to live happier lives. This is when our "inner glow" radiates to others we encounter. We would not suppose to say that one is merely encountering our hand when they shake it, or to imply that one has only met our face upon eye contact. We are seen by others as a totality of self and body. It is time that we see ourselves in this light as well.

Cooking with antioxidants is the only avenue to ensure that our bodies are nourished for beautiful skin. Antioxidant nutrients destroy free radicals, which damage collagen and the elasticity in our skin. Carrots are rich in vitamin A, a powerful antioxidant for skin health that is known to improve acne. Enjoy my Rainbow Salad on page 66, and remember that the nutrients are in the carrot skins, so do not peel them! My Pretty Poached Salmon (page 83) is also a great source of antioxidant-rich vitamin A, iron, and omega-3 fatty acids. Iron is an important nutrient that prevents dark circles under the eyes. Vitamin C is a potent antioxidant, and is found in cauliflower and Brussels sprouts, so indulge in my Sprouts and Flowers recipe on page 58 for a burst of antioxidants!

Enjoy nourishing your beautiful self with the following antioxidant-rich recipes for glowing skin!

Breakfast

Delicious Morning

serves 1

ingredients

1 cup barley cereal
1 cup soymilk vanilla enriched, or
substitute preferred milk
½ cup fresh berries (blueberries,
blackberries, or boysenberries) or
¼ cup dried berries

cooking instructions

Add all ingredients to cereal bowl and enjoy!

Fancy Yogurt

serves 1

Berries and yogurt with granola, mixed together for a delicious, healthy, and filling antioxidant breakfast. Enjoy!

ingredients

1 cup plain yogurt
5 raspberries
5 blackberries
¼ cup goji berries
⅓ cup granola
2 tablespoons honey

cooking instructions

Place yogurt in a bowl and top with raspberries, blackberries, goji berries, and granola. Drizzle with honey and serve.

Gourmet Yogurt

serves 1

ingredients

1½ cups of nonfat yogurt, plain
or vanilla
¼ cup goji berries
1 cup barley or oat cereal,
or granola

cooking instructions

Place yogurt in a large glass or cereal bowl. Add goji berries and cereal.

Organic Omelet

This omelet tastes as fabulous as it looks!

serves 2

ingredients

2 teaspoons extra virgin olive oil
2 tablespoons butter substitute
(margarine, or similar)
¼ cup diced red onion
8 cherry tomatoes, cut in half
2 small heirloom tomatoes,
chopped

2 artichoke hearts, chopped
2 cups baby spinach leaves
6 large egg whites, lightly beaten
4 large grapefruits, juiced
1 small loaf of corn bread

cooking instructions

Heat 1 teaspoon olive oil and 1 tablespoon butter substitute in a medium sauté pan over medium-high heat. Add onion and sauté for 2 minutes. Add tomatoes, artichoke hearts, and spinach and sauté for 1 minute more. Remove from heat and set aside.

Heat remaining 1 teaspoon olive oil and 1 tablespoon butter substitute in a nonstick omelet pan over medium heat. When they begin to sizzle, add egg whites and cook without stirring until whites begin to set. Using a spatula, push cooked egg whites up to allow raw whites to run underneath. When whites have nearly set completely, spoon vegetables over half the omelet and fold other half over. Cover and remove from heat. Allow to sit for 3 minutes before serving. Serve with fresh squeezed grapefruit juice and corn bread.

Fruity French Toast

serves 2

ingredients

Four 1-inch thick slices whole grain bread
1 small banana, peeled and thinly sliced
Nonstick cooking spray
2 large eggs
2 tablespoons milk

¼ cup macadamia nuts, coarsely chopped
¼ cup blueberries
¼ cup blackberries
¼ cup honey

cooking instructions

Slice a pocket into each piece of bread by inserting a small knife through the crust. Place banana slices into the bread pockets and set aside.

Spray a large skillet lightly with nonstick cooking spray and place over medium heat.

Whisk together the eggs and milk in a small bowl. Dip bread slices into egg mixture, letting it soak into both sides. Gently place into hot pan and cook until golden brown, about 2 minutes. Turn and cook until the other side is golden brown. Place on plates and sprinkle with macadamia nuts, blueberries, and blackberries. Drizzle with honey and serve hot.

Perfect Breakfast

serves 2

ingredients

2 eggs
2 large or 4 small spears green or
white asparagus
6 to 8 whole grain wheat crackers
Black pepper, to taste

cooking instructions

Place 4 inches of water in a small saucepan and bring to a boil over medium heat. Turn heat to medium low and add eggs. Simmer for 4 minutes for soft boiled, 5 to 6 minutes for medium, and 10 minutes for hard boiled.

Remove eggs from simmering water and add asparagus. Simmer for 1 minute then remove from water, drain, and place asparagus spears on a small plate with egg and crackers.

Lightly tap and crack the top of the eggshell with your teaspoon, and peel. Sprinkle egg with black pepper, and enjoy a perfect breakfast.

Peppery Palate Breakfast

serves 2

ingredients

2 large eggs
2 cups arugula
2 whole blackberries, for garnish
2 slices wheat bread, toasted and
cut in half on the diagonal
Blackberry jam
(I like the kind with seeds)
Cracked black pepper, to taste

Enjoy this wholesome breakfast flavored with hints of pepper. From the cracked black pepper garnish to the peppery taste of the arugula leaves, this leaves your palate pepper-happy!

cooking instructions

Bring a large saucepan of water to a boil over high heat. Carefully crack eggs into boiling water and let poach for 4 to 5 minutes.

Scatter arugula over plates. Place eggs over arugula and garnish with blackberries and cracked black pepper. Serve with toast and jam.

Variation: Substitute strawberry jam for blackberry jam; garnish with fresh strawberries.

Pink Antioxidant Breakfast

serves 2

ingredients

1 large pink grapefruit
Pinch of raw sugar or sugar
substitute
2 teabags (use your favorite
fruit-flavored tea)
2 tablespoons olive oil
6 large eggs whites, lightly beaten
6 boysenberries, mashed

Make someone you love blush with this lovely antioxidant breakfast that is pretty in pink!

cooking instructions

Cut grapefruit in half, and since nothing is ever perfectly halved, give the larger half to your love. Sprinkle with sugar, or sugar substitute for desired sweetness.

Place teabags in glass mugs, so that you can enjoy the pretty colored water created from the fruity tea. Pour boiling water over teabags and let steep for 3 to 4 minutes. Remove teabags.

Heat oil in a nonstick skillet over medium heat. Add egg whites and mashed boysenberries. Stir eggs for 5 to 7 minutes until scrambled and serve hot. Garnish with a couple of whole boysenberries for added beauty. The boysenberries will paint the white eggs pink!

Soups & Salads

Spicy Warm Tomato Soup

Spicy, warm tomato soup to heat your body and soul on a chilly day.

serves 4

ingredients

2 tablespoons extra virgin olive oil
½ cup onion, chopped
1 garlic clove, minced
1½ (28 ounce) cans crushed tomatoes
1½ cups vegetable broth
3 Roma tomatoes, chopped

Dash of Tabasco sauce
1 tablespoon chopped basil, for garnish
Pinch of black pepper

cooking instructions

Heat oil in a large pot over medium-high heat. Sauté onion and garlic until onion is tender, about 7 minutes. Stir in tomatoes and broth. Cover and simmer for 20 minutes, stirring frequently. Stir in Tabasco sauce.

Pour into bowl, garnish with basil, and with pepper before serving.

Antioxidant Fruit Soup

serves 4

ingredients

4 kiwis, peeled and diced
4 peaches, pitted and diced
1 small seedless watermelon, cut into 1-inch pieces
1 cup jicama sticks

cooking instructions

Reserve 20 pieces of watermelon; place remaining watermelon in a blender along with any accumulated watermelon juice. Puree until smooth.

Divide kiwi, peaches, jicama, and reserved watermelon pieces among 4 soup bowls. Pour watermelon puree over and serve.

Antioxidant Vegetable Salad

serves 4

Purchase spinach with the darkest green leaves you can find as they are highest in antioxidants. You'll be in antioxidant heaven!

ingredients

3 cups spinach leaves, washed
4 small red beets, peeled and thinly sliced
4 small yellow beets, peeled and thinly sliced
4 small orange beets, peeled and thinly sliced
1 Asian pear, sliced

12 small cremini or button mushrooms
5 hearts of palm, sliced
2 medium radishes, sliced
2 tablespoons raw sunflower seeds
2 tablespoons gogi berries
¼ cup dried cranberries
¼ cup purchased herb vinaigrette

cooking instructions

Arrange a bed of spinach among 4 salad plates. Arrange beets, pear, mushrooms, hearts of palm, and radishes attractively over. Sprinkle with sunflower seeds, gogi berries, and cranberries. Serve with your favorite herb vinaigrette.

Sprouts and Flowers

serves 2

Featured in Discovery Channel's Planet Green.

Garnish this beautiful dish with an edible flower from your garden!

ingredients

1 cup extra virgin olive oil
Juice from 1 lemon
½ cup rice vinegar
1 tablespoon flat-leaf parsley
Dash cayenne pepper
10 Brussels sprouts,
cut in half and steamed

2 Roma tomatoes, quartered
1 cup cauliflower florets
2 tablespoons sunflower seeds
2 tablespoons pumpkin seeds
1 cup prepared pumpkin,
butternut squash, or sweet
potatoes, cut into chunks

cooking instructions

Whisk together olive oil, lemon juice, rice vinegar, parsley, and cayenne pepper. Place the remaining ingredients in a medium bowl and toss with dressing. Serve at room temperature or chilled.

Hearts and Seeds

serves 4

Use whatever sprouts you like best to add to this colorful and delicious salad. Try radish or onion sprouts for a spicy bite. Lentil, wheat, sunflower, pumpkin, or sunflower sprouts are also great for a sweeter taste.

ingredients

3 tablespoons Dijon mustard, or to taste
3 tablespoons balsamic vinegar, or to taste
½ head red cabbage, shredded
6 hearts of palm, sliced into 1-inch pieces
1 cup water chestnuts, drained

1 cup sprouts
1 large pomegranate
(see page 80 for removing seeds)
Fresh ground black pepper, to taste

cooking instructions

Mix mustard and vinegar together in a small bowl until combined. Set aside. Divide cabbage, hearts of palm, water chestnuts, and sprouts among 4 salad plates. Drizzle with mustard mixture and sprinkle with pomegranate seeds. Sprinkle with black pepper and serve.

Candy Pear Salad

For a more salad-like dish, omit steaming the spinach and simply use it raw.

serves 4

ingredients

9 teaspoons butter
3 Japanese eggplants, cut in half lengthwise
⅓ cup packed golden brown sugar
4 Bartlett or Anjou pears, peeled and cut into cubes

8 cups s|
4 figs, cu
1 cup wa
½ cup ri

cooking instructions

Melt 2 teaspoons of the butter in a medium skillet over medium heat. Add eggplant cut-side down and cook until golden brown, about 4 minutes. Turn and cook until eggplant is cooked through, about 3 minutes more. Place eggplant on a plate and cover to keep warm.

Melt the remaining 7 teaspoons butter and brown sugar in the same skillet over medium heat. Add pears and bring to a simmer. Cook, stirring occasionally, until pears are golden and tender, about 8 minutes. Remove from heat.

Meanwhile, place spinach in a steamer basket over 1 inch of simmering water. Cover, reduce heat to low, and simmer for 1 minute.

Divide spinach among 4 salad plates and top with eggplant, pears, figs, walnuts, and rice cake crumbles.

Grape Leaves with Asparagus and Crumbled Feta

Grape leaves are available in jars packed in brine. Rinse and pat dry before using.

serves 2

ingredients

4 stalks white or green asparagus, stems uncut
6 grape leaves, rinsed and patted dry
½ cup feta cheese, crumbled
2 mint teabags
1 large lemon

cooking instructions

Steam asparagus. Divide asparagus and grape leaves among 2 plates. Divide feta cheese among plates. Place teabags in mugs. Pour boiling water over teabags and let steep for 3 to 4 minutes. Cut lemon in half. Squeeze some lemon juice into tea and over the grape leaves.

Many people are lactose intolerant, or have trouble digesting cheese or dairy products. If your condition is mild, there is a simple fix. Serve this antioxidant-rich recipe with soothing mint tea to counter-balance any disagreeable stomach issues caused by the feta cheese. The water that remains in the pot from the steamed asparagus has a beautiful sage green color, packed with antioxidant benefits, and also tastes delicious. Heat it up and add a touch of lemon for a wonderful tea beverage.

Rainbow Salad

serves 4

This salad is so colorful it's almost a shame to eat it! We want all the nutrients in the carrot skins so don't peel them, just wash them well.

ingredients

1 tablespoon balsamic vinegar
Juice from 1 lemon
2 tablespoons olive oil
3 stalks rainbow chard
1 cup cherry tomatoes
1 cup yellow pear tomatoes
1 red pepper, sliced

1 yellow pepper, sliced
1 green pepper, sliced
1 orange pepper, sliced
8 figs, quartered
4 small carrots, preferably rainbow carrots, sliced
3 hearts of palm, sliced

cooking instructions

Whisk together vinegar, lemon juice and olive oil until emulsified (mixture should have a silky texture). Set aside. Bring a medium pot of water to a boil over high heat. Place chard into boiling water for 30 seconds and remove. Rinse under cold water to keep it from overcooking and to cool. Place chard and remaining ingredients in a medium bowl and toss with dressing to coat. Serve immediately.

Heavenly Heirlooms

serves 1

ingredients

2 tablespoons olive oil
1 cup tiny heirloom tomatoes
(choose a medley of yellow,
orange, red, green, and deep
purple)
3 tablespoons Dijon mustard
3 tablespoons freshly squeezed
lime juice

½ teaspoon cracked black
pepper, plus more to taste
One 6-ounce can tuna packed
in water, drained
1 large beefsteak tomato,
top third cut off and insides
scooped out
Sprig of basil for garnish

Tomatoes come in a variety of beautiful colors, from deep purple cherry tomatoes, to yellow pear-shaped heirlooms, and each have a distinctive flavor. So, allow your palate to indulge in the wonders of this remarkable fruit.

cooking instructions

Heat 1 tablespoon of the olive oil in a medium saucepan over medium heat. Add heirloom tomatoes and cook, stirring frequently, until soft and "floppy". Set aside.

Mix the mustard, lime juice, remaining 1 tablespoon olive oil, and pepper in a small bowl. Add tuna and mix with a fork to flake tuna and combine. Remove heirloom tomatoes from saucepan with a slotted spoon and add to tuna mixture. Stir briefly to combine. Fill the beefsteak tomato with tuna-tomato mixture. Sprinkle pepper over. Garnish with basil.

Papaya Sour Cream Salad

serves 2

Papayas are the only natural source of papain, an effective natural digestive aid, which helps break down protein and cleanse the digestive track. This makes a decadent, yet digestively friendly, salad. If you can, use Hawaiian papaya, I think they're sweeter than the Mexican papaya.

ingredients

1 papaya, peeled, seeded
and cut into cubes
1 banana, peeled and
cut into 1-inch pieces
⅓ cup blueberries
1 cup sour cream
(low-fat or non-fat)

cooking instructions

Layer ingredients in a champagne flute and enjoy!

Flower Garden Menu

serves 2

Pick beautiful edible flowers from your garden, or take a walk into nature and pick some edible wildflowers. Get ready to go home and create a delicious bouquet!

ingredients

2 globe artichokes
½ cup balsamic vinegar
¼ cup mayonnaise
Juice from 4 pink grapefruit
Edible flowers for garnish such as nasturtiums, pansies, and borage

cooking instructions

Cut stems off artichokes. Using a serrated knife, cut off the top 2 inches to remove the "thorny" portion of the artichokes. Using scissors, cut off the tips of outer leaves to remove any thorns. Rinse thoroughly under running water to clean between each "petal". Place artichokes in a steamer basket over 2 inches of simmering water. Cover and steam until outer leaves are easily removed and flesh is tender, about 45 minutes, depending upon size.

Meanwhile, make sauce. Mix together vinegar and mayonnaise until creamy. Dress up your place setting with your freshly picked flowers. Serve artichoke with mayonnaise sauce, and enjoy with a tall glass of freshly squeezed grapefruit juice.

NOTE: To eat the artichoke heart, use a spoon to scrape out and discard the inedible fuzzy part, called "the choke". The heart can then be dipped in the same delicious sauce.

Salad Made of Gold

serves 2

ingredients

3 tablespoons olive oil,
plus more for greasing pan
2 skinless, bone-in 7-ounce
chicken breasts
1 teaspoon curry powder,
or to taste
1 tablespoon Dijon mustard
1 tablespoon mayonnaise

⅛ teaspoon paprika
2 medium golden beets, scrubbed,
peeled and diced
¼ cup golden raisins
3 stalks celery, chopped
1 small yellow onion, chopped
1 head radicchio leaves separated

cooking instructions

Preheat oven to 475°F. Lightly grease a small baking dish with a little olive oil.

Coat the chicken breasts with 1 tablespoon olive oil and sprinkle with curry powder. Bake until chicken is cooked through, 18 to 20 minutes. It's safer to have this dish a little overcooked rather than undercooked, because the dressing will add moisture to the chicken. Remove from heat and let chicken cool enough to safely handle. Tear chicken into small pieces.

Whisk together the remaining 2 tablespoons olive oil, mustard, mayonnaise, and paprika in a large bowl. Add beets, raisins, celery, onion, and chicken and toss to coat.

Place spoonfuls of salad mixture into radicchio lettuce cups and serve.

Cantaloupe and Yogurt Salad

serves 4

The cantaloupe becomes the salad bowl in a pleasant twist on the 1893 classic Waldorf salad. Serve it for dessert!

ingredients

1 cantaloupe, cut into quarters
6 tablespoons plain nonfat yogurt
2 tablespoons freshly squeezed
lemon juice
Ground black pepper, to taste
1 cup walnuts, toasted (choose any
nut you prefer, or go "nuts" and use
a couple different types!)

1 cup celery, sliced
½ cup red seedless grapes
½ cup black seedless grapes
⅓ cup golden raisins
1 Pink Lady apple, cored and
chopped

cooking instructions

Remove seeds and a little extra flesh from the cantaloupe so you can use it as salad bowls. Set aside.

Mix together yogurt, lemon juice, and pepper in a large bowl. Add remaining ingredients and toss to coat with dressing. Spoon into your cantaloupe bowls and enjoy your fruity bowl-turned-dessert!

Citrus Crabmeat Salad

serves 4

This blend of tangy pink-fleshed grapefruit, blood oranges, and crabmeat tastes as exquisite as it looks. If you are cooking on a budget, replace real crabmeat with imitation crabmeat. Crabmeat can be found at the seafood counter of your local market.

ingredients

1 cup nonfat mayonnaise
¼ cup Italian-style salad dressing (I love Bernstein's Restaurant Recipe)
3 tablespoons nonfat sour cream
2 tablespoons lemon juice
½ teaspoon dried oregano
Ground black pepper, to taste
½ red onion, chopped

½ green bell pepper, diced
1 stalk celery, diced
11 ounces crabmeat, flaked
2 pink grapefruit, peeled and cut into segments
4 blood oranges, peeled and cut into segments

cooking instructions

Place mayonnaise, salad dressing, sour cream, lemon juice, oregano, and pepper in a small bowl and stir to combine.

Combine onion, green bell pepper, celery, and crab meat in a medium bowl. Add sour cream mixture to crab mixture and toss lightly to coat. Cover and let chill for 1 hour.

Divide grapefruit and orange segments among 4 salad bowls, to make a bed of bright pink and deep red delicious. Spoon chilled crabmeat salad over and serve.

Fish & Seafood Entrées

Warm Grapefruit Ahi Tuna Salad

serves 4

ingredients

12 ounces sushi-grade ahi tuna
1 small head radicchio or
½ head red cabbage, torn
1 pink grapefruit, cut into segments
12 dates, pitted and thinly sliced
⅓ cup rosemary, pea, onion, alfalfa, or other sprouts
2 stalks celery, sliced

8 brown turkey figs, quartered
Juice from 1 lemon
2 tablespoons extra virgin olive oil

cooking instructions

Heat a cast iron skillet over high heat until it begins to smoke. Add tuna and cook for 1 minute on each side. Remove from heat and cut into 1-inch pieces.

Divide radicchio leaves among 4 salad plates. Top with grapefruit, dates, sprouts, celery, figs, and tuna.

Whisk together lemon juice and olive oil and drizzle over salads.

Pomegranate Tuna

Featured on
MySkinAffair.com

serves 1

ingredients

1 medium pomegranate
One 6-ounce can chunk white tuna
in water, drained
4 radicchio leaves
¼ cup raw almonds
1 teaspoon chives, chopped
Lemon wedge for garnish

cooking instructions

Using a sharp knife cut the pomegranate into two or three pieces. With the sea of ruby red seeds facing away from you, use your thumbs to push the pomegranate pieces inside out, away from you, over a bowl. Once the pomegranate is popped inside out, simply pick off the seeds.

Place radicchio leaves on a plate. Flake tuna with a fork and place over radicchio. Sprinkle with almonds, pomegranate seeds, and chives. Garnish with lemon wedge and serve.

What could be prettier than tuna on a bed of purple-red radicchio leaves and ruby red pomegranate seeds? Many stores carry pomegranate seeds in their fresh produce section. If seeding them yourself, wear an old shirt or an apron to protect your clothes, and latex or rubber gloves to keep your hands from turning magenta. Use a plastic cutting board as pomegranates will stain wood. The pomegranate seeds can stain the grout on your counter, too.

Tart Tuna

serves 2

The flavor of the wine and berries infuse the tuna with a deep sweetness. The alcohol will cook off, so don't worry your skin with any possible dehydration.

ingredients

2 teaspoons olive oil
One 10 to 12 ounce ahi tuna steak
½ cup red wine
½ cup blackberries
½ cup pitted black cherries
½ cup dried cranberries

cooking instructions

Heat olive oil in a medium, heavy skillet (preferably cast iron) over high heat. When oil just starts to smoke, add tuna and cook for 1 to 2 minutes just to sear. Turn and cook for 1 to 2 minutes more. Place tuna on a plate and set aside.

Reduce heat to medium high, add red wine, and bring to a boil. Add blackberries, cherries, and cranberries and let simmer until fruit is soft and mixture has thickened, about 10 minutes. Spoon antioxidant berry sauce over tuna before serving.

Pretty Poached Salmon

serves 2

ingredients

⅓ cup water
Two 5-ounce salmon fillets
Sea salt
Freshly ground black pepper
20 blackberries, reserve
2 for garnish
20 raspberries
¼ cup honey
6 leaves radicchio

This is a delicious sight to behold and has a sensationally flavorful taste. Chop one or two boysenberries and raspberries and stir into the pureed berry mixture to add texture and create a tart, melt-in-your-mouth sensation that will make your lips pucker up. Enjoy this antioxidant-rich recipe with someone special, this is definitely a romantic recipe for two!

cooking instructions

Place water in a small sauté pan over high heat and bring to a boil. Place salmon in boiling water, sprinkle with salt and pepper, and cover tightly with a lid or with foil. Reduce heat to low and let cook for 10 to 12 minutes until salmon is cooked through.

Meanwhile, make the berry glaze. Puree 18 blackberries, raspberries, and honey in a blender or small food processor until nearly smooth. Set aside.

Place radicchio on plates. Remove salmon from pan and place over radicchio. Pour berry glaze over salmon and garnish with remaining 2 blackberries.

Shrimp Scampi

serves 3 to 4

ingredients

1 pound frozen jumbo shrimp
⅓ cup margarine, or butter
substitute
1 garlic clove, minced
Juice and zest from 1 lemon
Dash of cayenne pepper
2 tablespoons parsley, chopped

cooking instructions

Place shrimp in a strainer, running tepid water over it until thawed.

Melt margarine in a large skillet over medium heat. Add shrimp and garlic, and cook until just heated through. Remove from heat and stir in lemon juice, lemon zest, cayenne pepper, and parsley. Serve hot.

Scallop and Beet Tower

serves 2

Let your tower stand tall, eating it layer by layer, or knock it down and enjoy blending your bites!

ingredients

1 tablespoon olive oil
8 large scallops, about 2-inch diameter
2 golden beets, about 2-inch diameter, peeled and thinly sliced
2 red beets, about 2-inch diameter, peeled and thinly sliced
1 tablespoon butter or margarine
½ teaspoon chives, minced

2 shallots, finely chopped
1 cup your favorite white wine
¼ cup golden raisins
Pure red and golden beet juice

cooking instructions

Heat olive oil in a medium skillet over medium-high heat. Add scallops and cook without moving until golden brown, about 2 minutes. Turn scallops over and cook until lightly browned. Place scallops on a plate and cover to keep them warm.

Add golden beets to skillet and cook until tender, about 3 minutes. Place golden beets on a plate and cover to keep warm. Add red beets to skillet and cook until tender, about 3 minutes. Place red beets on a plate and cover to keep warm.

Add butter, chives, and shallots to skillet and sauté until lightly golden, about 3 minutes. Add white wine (the alcohol will cook off, so don't worry about your skin or possible dehydration!) and bring to a boil over high heat. Reduce heat and let simmer until wine has reduced by half. Remove from heat and stir in raisins.

Create your tower by making a stack of one slice of red beet, one slice of golden beet, and one scallop. Then add another slice of golden beet, another slice of red beet, and finish with another scallop. Drizzle each stack with wine sauce and garnish with raisins. Admire its beauty, then nourish yourself with its nutritious, health-giving properties.

Drink with a glass of pure red and golden beet juice. Use a straw to reduce teeth staining.

Dover Sole with Carrot-Ginger Puree

serves 2

ingredients

2 tablespoons extra virgin olive oil
¾ pound Dover sole fillets
(about 4 fillets)
Cracked black pepper, to taste
4 carrots, unpeeled, scrubbed, and
coarsely chopped
½ inch piece of ginger root,
unpeeled
Parsley leaves, for garnish

cooking instructions

Preheat oven to 425°F.

Place olive oil in a shallow baking dish. Add fillets and turn to coat all sides. Sprinkle with cracked pepper. Bake until fillets flake easily and are cooked through, 10 to 15 minutes.

Place carrots in a steamer basket over 2 inches of simmering water. Cover and steam over low heat for 3 to 5 minutes. Remove from heat.

Place carrots and ginger in the bowl of a food processor and blend until perfectly smooth.

To serve, spoon some carrot-ginger puree on a plate and lay filet over. Garnish with parsley and serve.

Hearty Halibut

serves 2

Halibut has a light, delicate flavor with a hearty texture. It also has omega-3 fatty acids that benefit the cardiovascular system, by helping to prevent erratic heart rhythms, and making blood less likely to clot inside arteries—the most common cause of heart attacks. This is one big-hearted fish!

ingredients

2 tablespoons extra virgin olive oil
4 tablespoons of margarine
or other butter substitute
4 shallots, chopped
6 garlic cloves, minced
1½ cups cherry, grape,
or pear tomatoes
2 cups baby spinach leaves

Two 5- to 7-ounce halibut fillets
2 tablespoons freshly grated
parmesan cheese
1 lemon, cut into wedges

cooking instructions

Heat 1 tablespoon olive oil and 2 tablespoons margarine in a medium-size saucepan over medium heat. Add shallots, garlic, and tomatoes and sauté until the tomatoes and skins have softened and the aroma of garlic and shallots awakens your senses, about 10 minutes. Add spinach and stir. Cover, turn heat to low, and let cook while you prepare the halibut.

Heat remaining 1 tablespoon olive oil and 2 tablespoons margarine in a medium skillet over medium-high heat. Add the halibut and let cook without moving until golden brown, about 5 minutes. Turn and continue cooking until the other side is golden and fish is cooked through, about 4 minutes.

To serve, spoon tomato-spinach mixture equally on plates and place halibut over. Sprinkle with freshly grated parmesan cheese and serve with lemon wedges.

Sautéed Scallops in a Caramelized 'Camelot'

serves 4

ingredients

2 teaspoons plus
1 tablespoon olive oil
⅓ cup packed brown sugar
4 ripe red pears,
cut in half lengthwise and cored
12 large scallops
(about 1½ pounds)
Ground black pepper, to taste
One 7-ounce bag baby spinach

Break the rules and enjoy your fish with fruit, instead of vegetables, in this delightfully creative recipe. Just like King Arthur's Camelot, this dish's baked scallops with caramelized pears will transport you to a heavenly utopia, so be sure to dine at a round table!

cooking instructions

Heat 2 teaspoons olive oil in a large skillet over medium heat. Place brown sugar on a plate. Press the cut side of the pears in brown sugar and coat thickly. Place pears, sugar-side down, in skillet and cook for 5 to 7 minutes. Lower heat if sugar starts to burn.

Add ½ cup water to skillet and bring to a boil. Cover, reduce heat to low, and simmer for 8 to 10 minutes, adding more water as necessary. Remove pears from skillet and cover to keep warm. Continue simmering the sauce until very thick. Set aside.

Meanwhile, place remaining 1 tablespoon olive oil in another large skillet over high heat. Add scallops and cook without moving until golden brown, about 2 minutes. Turn and cook on other side until golden and cooked through, 1 to 2 minutes. Season with pepper and remove from heat.

To serve, divide spinach among 4 dinner plates and lay 3 scallops on each plate. Cut pears into chunks and arrange around scallops. Drizzle sauce from the pears over all.

Mahi Mahi... Healthy Healthy

serves 2

ingredients

1 green bell pepper, sliced
1 yellow bell pepper, sliced
1 red bell pepper, sliced
1 orange bell pepper, sliced
½ medium red onion, cut into 1-inch pieces

8 ounces medium-size mushrooms (use your favorite, any will do!), cut in quarters
2 tablespoons olive oil
1 tablespoon soy sauce
Two 5- to 6-ounce mahi mahi fillets

cooking instructions

Place peppers, onion, and mushrooms in a large baking dish and drizzle with 1 tablespoon olive oil and soy sauce, tossing to coat. Cook at 375°F for 15 minutes, until tops just begin to char.

Place remaining 1 tablespoon olive oil in a small baking dish. Add fillets to baking dish, turning to coat both sides. Bake until cooked through, about 12 minutes.

Place mahi mahi on top of a bed of roasted vegetables to serve.

> The mild, sweet flavor of the mahi mahi is in sharp contrast to the intensity of the nutritional value in the fish. It is packed heavily with protein, and found year-round at your local grocery store.

White Wine Shellfish... Delish

serves 2

ingredients

One 12-ounce package linguini pasta
3 tablespoons olive oil
1 tablespoon unsalted butter
4 white pearl onions, diced
2 shallots, diced
½ cup white wine
6 large shrimp, peeled and deveined

6 mussels, beards removed
6 medium clams or 12 small clams
2 Roma tomatoes, diced
½ cup heavy cream
1 tablespoon tarragon

cooking instructions

Bring a large pot of water to a boil over high heat. Add pasta and cook according to package directions. Drain in a large colander under warm running water and toss with 2 tablespoons olive oil.

Heat remaining 1 tablespoon olive oil and butter in a medium saucepan over medium-high heat. Add onions and shallots and cook, stirring constantly until soft, about 4 minutes. Add white wine and bring to a boil. Add shrimp, mussels, clams, and tomatoes. Cover, reduce heat, and simmer until shrimp is cooked through and mussels and clams have opened up.

Stir in cream and tarragon and bring to a boil. Remove from heat and serve in bowls, so the shellfish bathes in the delightful white wine sauce.

Shellfish in white wine sauce is a simple recipe with a sophisticated taste. In just minutes, you are ready to serve a sumptuous entrée.

Chilean Sea Bass and Vegetables

This deliciously mild fish is perfectly complimented by sweet pearl onions and baby carrots.

serves 2

ingredients

2 tablespoons olive oil
Two 5- to 7-ounce
Chilean sea bass fillets
6 small pearl onions, diced
2 cloves garlic, mashed
4 shallots, diced
6 baby carrots
6 spears white asparagus

cooking instructions

Preheat oven to 350°F. Place 1 tablespoon of the olive oil in a shallow baking dish. Add fillets to baking dish, turning to coat both sides. Bake until fish is throughly cooked through and flakes easily with a fork, about 18 minutes.

Meanwhile, heat remaining 1 tablespoon olive oil in a skillet over medium-high heat. Add onions, garlic, and shallots. Sauté, stirring frequently, until onions are a lightly golden.

Place carrots and asparagus in a steamer basket over 1 inch of simmering water. Cover and steam until cooked through, about 3 minutes.

Place sea bass on plates and spoon onion mixture over. Serve with carrots and asparagus.

Meat, Poultry & Vegetable Entrées

Delectable Duck

serves 4

ingredients

One 5 pound duck
Salt
2 cups dried cranberries
⅓ cup orange juice
2 large oranges, peeled and
chopped
¼ cup chopped parsley
¼ cup rosemary, cut into smaller
pieces with sprigs kept on stalks

cooking instructions

Preheat oven to 400°F. Remove neck from cavity and rinse duck under cold running water. Pat dry with paper towels. Tuck wings behind duck. Tie drumsticks together with kitchen twine. Place duck on a rack inside a roasting pan and sprinkle generously with salt. Roast duck until cooked through and an instant-read thermometer inserted into the thickest part of the thigh registers 165°F. Remove from oven and cover loosely with foil to keep warm.

Meanwhile, place cranberries and orange juice in a medium saucepan and bring to a boil over high heat. Reduce heat, cover, and simmer until cranberries are soft, about 3 minutes. Stir in oranges, parsley, and rosemary and cook for 2 minutes.

Place duck on a serving platter and spoon cranberry mixture over.

Meatloaf with Wild Rice

serves 4

ingredients

Nonstick cooking spray
1 cup minced yellow onion
4 tablespoons chopped parsley
4 teaspoons chopped basil
1 pound lean ground beef,
preferably grass-fed
½ cup breadcrumbs
1 large egg, lightly beaten
1 teaspoon salt

1 teaspoon pepper
¼ cup tomato sauce
One 8-ounce package prepared
wild rice
One 8-ounce package prepared
brown rice
1 garlic clove, minced
Juice from 1 lemon

cooking instructions

Preheat oven to 350°F. Generously spray a 6-inch loaf pan with nonstick cooking spray.

Place onion, 4 tablespoons parsley, 4 teaspoons basil, ground beef, breadcrumbs, egg, salt, and pepper in a medium mixing bowl and combine with clean hands until very well mixed. Pack into prepared loaf pan. Spread tomato sauce over top and bake until cooked through, about 55 minutes. Let cool for 10 minutes before slicing.

Meanwhile, heat wild rice and brown rice according to package directions. Place in a bowl and toss with garlic, and lemon juice. Serve rice with slices of meatloaf.

Peppered Persimmon Steak

serves 1

ingredients

Two 6- to 7-ounce New York,
market, or strip steaks
Black pepper
1 persimmon, sliced into ¼-inch
pieces
Pomegranate seeds
1 teaspoon small rosemary sprigs

cooking instructions

Preheat broiler.

Sprinkle steaks with pepper. Broil steaks until browned on top, 5 to
7 minutes. Turn over and place persimmon slices on top. Continue
broiling until steaks are cooked to desired doneness, between 5 to 12
minutes, depending on thickness.

Serve steaks with pomegranate seeds and rosemary sprinkled over.

Tropical Lamb

serves 2

ingredients

Enjoy a sensational tropical salsa and infuse your lamb with mouth-watering, antioxidant-rich fruits and vegetables. Try halibut or any other mild white fish instead of lamb, if you like. This recipe will make extra salsa so try the leftovers on top of an omelet with cottage cheese and toast. Yum!

1 rack of lamb
1 tablespoon olive oil
Sea salt
Freshly ground black pepper
¼ pineapple, peeled and diced
2 kiwis, peeled and diced
2 mangos, peeled, seeded and diced
1 small red bell pepper, diced

1 small red onion, diced
2 plum tomatoes, diced
2 tablespoons chopped mint leaves
1 tablespoon chopped cilantro, or to taste
2 cloves garlic, minced, optional

cooking instructions

Preheat oven to 475°F. Slice rack of lamb into individual chops (2 bones per chop) and rub with olive oil. Sprinkle with salt and pepper and place on a baking sheet. Roast until nicely browned, about 7 minutes. Turn and roast, until the other side is also browned, 5 minutes more. Remove from oven and cover with foil to keep warm. Let lamb rest for 5 minutes before serving.

Meanwhile, make the salsa. Mix pineapple, kiwis, mangos, bell pepper, onion, tomatoes, mint, and cilantro together. Season to taste with salt and pepper. Add garlic if desired. To serve, spoon salsa over lamb.

Pining for Poultry

serves 2

ingredients

2 skinless, boneless chicken breasts
8 garlic cloves, mashed
1 tablespoon extra virgin olive oil
6 spears green or white asparagus
1 cup cauliflower florets
2 cups broccoli florets

cooking instructions

Preheat oven to 425°F. Pat chicken breast dry with paper towels.

Mash together garlic and olive oil, then spread over top of chicken breasts. Place in a shallow baking dish and roast until chicken is cooked through, 15 to 20 minutes.

Meanwhile, place asparagus, cauliflower, and broccoli in a steamer basket over 1 inch of simmering water. Cover, reduce heat to low, and simmer until tender, about 7 minutes. Serve hot with chicken.

Chile Pepper Chicken

serves 2

ingredients

Nonstick cooking spray
Juice from 2 lemons
3 tablespoons Dijon mustard
Black pepper, to taste
6 chicken wings
2 jalapeño peppers, seeded and
minced

cooking instructions

Preheat oven to 425°F. Spray a baking sheet with a generous amount of nonstick cooking spray.

Whisk together lemon juice and mustard in a medium bowl. Add pepper. Set aside half of mixture in a ramekin.

Add chicken wings to remaining mixture and toss to coat. Place wings on prepared baking sheet, place jalapeño peppers atop chicken wings, and roast until skin is crispy and golden, about 40 minutes. Serve wings hot with sauce for dipping.

Gently Curried Lamb

serves 10

This meal is to be enjoyed with some great company. Perhaps at a barbecue at your local park, or outside on a lazy Sunday at the barbecue at your local park, or at home in your yard. Skewered lamb with curry seasoning is a social and playful way to experience a complicated taste. Serve with my Lime Chutney (page 130).

ingredients

2 pounds boneless leg of lamb, cut into 1-inch squares
1 large red onion, cut into 1-inch pieces, layers separated
1/3 cup extra virgin olive oil
1 to 2 tablespoons curry powder, or to taste
10 bamboo skewers, soaked in water for 10 minutes to prevent burning

cooking instructions

Preheat grill on high.

Combine lamb, onion, and olive oil in a medium bowl. Sprinkle with curry powder and toss to combine. Place alternating pieces of lamb and onions on bamboo skewers.

Grill over high heat, turning to cook on all sides, until meat is just a little pink at the center, about 12 minutes.

Serve with Lime Chutney (see page 130), which can double as a chips dip if you include some potato chips into the mix for some crispy summer fun!

Filet Mignon and Figs

serves 2

ingredients

1 tablespoon olive oil
Two 4-ounce filet mignons, about
1-inch thick
¼ cup red wine
7 medium black mission or brown
turkey figs

cooking instructions

Heat olive oil in a small skillet over medium-high heat. Add filets and cook for 2 to 4 minutes on each side, depending on desired doneness. Place filets on a plate and cover to keep warm. Turn heat to high and add red wine. Bring to a boil, stirring to loosen up any brown bits that have stuck to the bottom of the pan, until wine has reduced to about 2 tablespoons, about 5 minutes.

Place 5 of the figs in the bowl of a food processor or blender. Add reduced wine to the bowl and puree until smooth. Cut remaining 2 figs into wedges. Serve steaks with fig puree and wedges.

Veal atop Bed of Warm Chard

serves 2

ingredients

2 tablespoons extra virgin olive oil
Two 3-ounce veal medallions,
½ inch thick (or 4 medallions
to serve 2)
2 bunches chard, stems removed
1 cup cremini or porcini
mushrooms, chopped into chunks
4 shallots, minced
1 medium red onion, chopped

6 garlic cloves, minced
1 cup your favorite sweet
or dessert wine

cooking instructions

Heat 1 tablespoon olive oil in a medium skillet over medium-high heat. Add veal and cook until browned, 2 to 3 minutes. Turn and cook for 2 to 3 minutes more, until just barely pink in the center. Place veal on a plate and cover to keep warm.

Place chard in a steamer basket over 1 inch of simmering water. Cover and steam until just wilted, about 2 minutes.

In the same skillet used to cook the veal, heat remaining 1 tablespoon olive oil over medium heat. Add mushrooms, shallots, red onion, and garlic, and sauté until golden, about 7 minutes. Stir in wine and simmer for 15 minutes.

To serve, divide chard among 2 plates. Place veal over and spoon mushroom sauce over all.

Variation: Cook 2 whole shitake mushrooms with heavy stems, and add to the wine and mushroom sauce and serve for special presentation.

Pork Chops and Savory White Bean Puree

Meat never tasted so sweet! The delicious sugary crunch of Pink Lady apples perfectly complements the soft, savory puree of white beans in this delicious pork recipe.

ingredients

Two 5-ounce boneless pork chops
One 14.5-ounce can white beans, drained and rinsed
1 Pink Lady apple
(or any sweet apple you prefer), cored and thinly sliced

cooking instructions

Preheat broiler.

Place pork chops under broiler and cook for 5 to 7 minutes. Turn and cook until browned and cooked through, about 5 minutes more.

Meanwhile, place white beans in the bowl of a food processor or blender. Process until smooth. Place in a small saucepan over medium heat and cook until heated through.

Serve pork chops with white beans and apple slices.

Cherry and Turkey Meatball Angel Hair Pasta

serves 2

ingredients

10 Bing cherries, stemmed and pitted
¼ cup granulated sugar
½ pound ground turkey
1 large egg
1 slice whole wheat bread, torn into tiny pieces
3 garlic cloves, minced

2 shallots, minced
½ teaspoon plus 1 tablespoon olive oil
One 8-ounce package angel hair pasta

This romantic dish ought to be shared with the one you love. The sweetness of the cherries complements the rustic taste of the turkey meatballs, and enjoyed with angelic pasta creates a complex taste. Enjoy!

cooking instructions

Place cherries and sugar in a saucepan with ¾ cup water. Bring to a boil over medium heat, reduce heat, and simmer for 10 to 15 minutes. Cherries should be soft but still maintain their shape.

Meanwhile, mix together ground turkey, egg, bread, garlic, shallots, and ½ teaspoon olive oil. Roll turkey meatballs using clean hands into size you desire.

Heat remaining 1 tablespoon olive oil in a large skillet over medium-high heat. Add meatballs and brown on all sides, making sure they are cooked all the way through.

Bring a large pot of water to a boil over high heat. Add pasta and cook according to package directions. Drain in a colander and place in a large bowl. Add poached cherries, along with their cooking liquid, and lightly toss. Place meatballs on top, and serve.

Salsa and Tortilla

serves 4

ingredients

4 whole grain flour tortillas
1 cup prepared broad or fava beans
1 cup prepared pinto beans
2 Roma tomatoes, chopped
4 shallots, thinly sliced
1 small red onion, chopped

2 avocados, seeded and chopped
1 large cucumber, peeled and diced
3 garlic cloves, minced

cooking instructions

Place 1 tortilla on each of 4 dinner plates and top with beans.

Combine remaining ingredients in a medium bowl. Spoon over beans and serve.

Rib-Eye on Cauliflower

serves 2

ingredients

1½ teaspoon teaspoons
curry powder
Two 10- 12-ounce rib-eye steaks
1 tablespoon olive oil
½ head white cauliflower, chopped
¼ cup golden raisins
¼ cup brown raisins

The earth tones of the curried cauliflower and golden raisins add a flavor of nature to this unique steak recipe. This recipe calls for white cauliflower, but you may substitute purple, green, or even pink. I enjoy the hearty taste of cold steak and cauliflower. If you have leftovers this delicious dish tastes just as lovely served cold.

¼ cup dried currants
Seeds from ½ pomegranate
(see page 80 for directions on removing seeds)

cooking instructions

Preheat broiler.

Sprinkle ½ teaspoon curry powder on both sides of the steaks and rub into surface of meat. Broil steaks for 8 to 12 minutes on each side, or until desired doneness is reached.

Meanwhile, heat olive oil in a large skillet over medium-high heat. Add remaining 1 teaspoon curry powder, cauliflower, raisins, and currants. Sauté, stirring frequently, until curry has painted the white cauliflower florets a pretty yellow color, about 7 minutes.

To serve, divide cauliflower between 2 plates. Place steaks over. Sprinkle with pomegranate seeds. Place any leftovers covered in the refrigerator, to enjoy the following day for lunch.

Broad Bean Dish

serves 2

The parsley beautifully counteracts the odorous effects of the garlic.

ingredients

1 tablespoon extra virgin olive oil, plus more as needed
8 ounces mushrooms, sliced
3 cloves garlic, minced
6 shallots, finely sliced
1 medium red onion, diced
One 14-ounce can broad beans, drained and rinsed

One 5-ounce bag arugula
⅓ cup chopped parsley
Juice from 1 lemon

cooking instructions

Heat olive oil in a large sauté pan over medium heat. Add all the mushrooms and cook until golden, about 3 minutes. Add the garlic, shallots, and onion, and cook, stirring constantly, until garlic is light golden, about 4 minutes.

Add broad beans and cook until just heated through. Add arugula and parsley and continue cooking until arugula has just wilted. Remove from heat and stir in lemon juice. Drizzle with a little more olive oil before serving, if desired. Extra virgin, unrefined olive oil is a great source of vitamin D.

Kale Layered Lasagna

serves 6

Kale, a powerful antioxidant, is more than just a beautiful leaf. Kale is high in fiber and simply chewing it activates detoxifying enzymes in the liver. It contains high levels of vitamin A—important nutrients for vision, too. The bitterness of the kale is subdued by the mild creaminess of the ricotta cheese, creating a subtle play of flavors on your palate.

ingredients

3 tablespoons olive oil
One 12-ounce package lasagna noodles
1 bunch kale, chopped
⅓ cup chopped mushrooms
1⅓ chopped cup onion
1 tablespoon minced garlic
1 cup ricotta cheese
4 tablespoons shredded Romano cheese

¼ teaspoon sea salt
¼ teaspoon dried oregano
¼ teaspoon dried basil
¼ teaspoon ground black pepper
⅓ large egg
2 cups prepared marinara sauce
16 ounces shredded mozzarella cheese
½ cup grated Parmesan cheese

cooking instructions

Preheat oven to 350°F. Coat a 9x13-inch baking dish with 1 tablespoon of the olive oil and set aside.

Bring a large pot of water to a boil over high heat. Place lasagna noodles in boiling water and cook according to the package directions. Drain in a colander. Set aside.

Using the same pot, add 2 cups of water and bring to a boil over high heat. Add kale and cook until wilted and soft, about 5 minutes. Drain well, pressing to release excess water. Place kale on several paper towels and roll up to squeeze out remaining water. Set aside.

Heat remaining 2 tablespoons olive oil in a large skillet over medium-high heat. Sauté mushrooms, onion, and garlic until onions are tender and translucent.

Combine ricotta and Romano cheeses, kale, salt, oregano, basil, pepper, and egg in a large bowl. Stir in mushroom mixture.

Place a quarter of the lasagna noodles over the bottom of the prepared baking dish. Spread with one-third of the cheese mixture. Spoon a half cup of the marinara sauce over. Sprinkle with a quarter of the mozzarella and Parmesan cheeses. Repeat layering two more times. Place remaining lasagna noodles on top. Spoon remaining marinara sauce over noodles and sprinkle with the rest of the mozzarella cheese. Cover loosely with foil and bake for 45 minutes. Uncover and bake until top is golden brown and bubbly, about 15 minutes more.

Heavenly Pasta

serves 4

ingredients

One 12-ounce package angel hair
pasta
4 tablespoons extra virgin olive oil
1½ cups prepared marinara sauce
1 yellow bell pepper, cut into
1-inch pieces

1 bunch asparagus spears, cut into
2-inch pieces
One 10-ounce can artichoke
hearts packed in water, drained
Black pepper, to taste

cooking instructions

Bring a large pot of water to a boil over high heat. Add pasta and cook
according to package directions. Drain in a large colander under warm
running water and toss with 2 tablespoons olive oil.

Meanwhile, heat marinara in a small saucepan. When hot, remove from
heat and cover to keep warm.

Heat remaining 2 tablespoons olive oil in a medium saucepan over
medium heat. Add yellow bell pepper, asparagus, and artichoke hearts
and cook until they begin to turn golden. Add to pasta and toss to
combine. Place pasta in pasta bowls and serve with sauce.

BWT (Bacon, Whole Wheat, and Tomatoes)

Whole wheat pasta is a healthy alternative to white pasta, and is easy to find in the pasta section of your local market.

serves 4

ingredients

One 16-ounce package whole wheat pasta
2 tablespoons olive oil
20 cherry, pear, or grape tomatoes, cut in half
¼ chopped cup basil
5 slices bacon, cooked and crumbled

cooking instructions

Bring a large pot of water to a boil over high heat. Add pasta and cook according to package directions. Drain in a colander and toss with 1 tablespoon olive oil. Set aside.

Heat remaining 1 tablespoon olive oil in a medium skillet over medium-high heat. Add tomatoes and basil and cook, stirring occasionally, until tomatoes are soft, about 5 minutes. Stir in crumbled bacon and remove from heat.

Spoon cherry tomatoes over pasta to serve.

Side Dishes & Snacks

Artichoke Delight

serves 2

ingredients

2 globe artichokes
1 sprig fresh rosemary
3 cups fresh cranberries
3 tablespoons sugar or sugar substitute, or to taste
½ cup almonds, chopped

Artichokes are beautiful flower foods and are also intense aphrodisiacs. So, cook this delightful dish for someone who makes your heart flutter. Love itself is a recipe for beauty, for nothing makes your skin glow quite like love.

cooking instructions

Place 1 inch of water in a large saucepan and bring to a boil over high heat.

Using a serrated knife, cut off the top 2 inches to remove the "thorny" portion of the artichokes. Snap off the small leaves around the bottom of the artichoke. Using scissors, cut the tips of outer leaves to remove any thorns. Trim stem.

Place artichokes and rosemary in boiling water and cover. Reduce heat to low and let simmer until outer leaves are easily removed and flesh is tender, 30 to 45 minutes. Remove from saucepan, drain, and let cool for 5 minutes.

Meanwhile, place cranberries, sugar, and ¼ cup water in a medium saucepan over medium-high heat. Bring to a simmer and cover. Let simmer until most of the cranberries have popped, about 20 minutes. Remove from heat and mash cranberries with a wooden spoon. Stir in chopped almonds.

Cut artichokes in half lengthwise. Scoop out any choke from the center of the artichokes with a spoon. Serve artichokes with cranberry dipping sauce.

Get ready to dip your artichoke in antioxidant decadence! Chopped almonds add crunch and rosemary compliments the tart sweetness of the cranberries.

Steamed Spinach Toast

serves 2

ingredients

4 slices whole grain bread, toasted
¼ cup raw, chunky or smooth
almond butter
3 cups spinach leaves, rinsed
Dash ground cinnamon
¼ cup of golden raisins or currants

You may well want to use a knife and fork for this delicious antioxidant-rich recipe.

cooking instructions

Place spinach leaves in a steamer over 1 inch of simmering water. Cover and steam for 2 minutes over low heat. Remove from heat and let spinach drain on paper towels.

Spread raw almond butter over slices of warm toast. Place spinach on top of toast and sprinkle with a dash of cinnamon and raisins. Serve while spinach is still warm.

Fun Rice

serves 4

A simple recipe with a surprisingly complex and delicious taste!

ingredients

½ cup pine nuts
5 spears asparagus, chopped
½ cup small cauliflower florets
2 cups hot, cooked brown rice
2 cups hot, cooked wild rice
½ cup pecan halves

¼ cup dried cranberries
Seeds from 1 pomegranate
(see page 80 for removing seeds)
Pinch of fresh thyme
Black pepper, to taste
2 teaspoons minced flat-leaf
parsley

cooking instructions

Preheat oven to 350°F. Place pine nuts on a baking sheet and toast until lightly golden, about 6 minutes. Let cool.

Place asparagus and cauliflower in a steamer basket over approximately 1½ inches of simmering water. Cover and steam for 3 to 5 minutes over low heat. Remove from heat.

Place pine nuts, asparagus, and remaining ingredients in a medium bowl and stir to combine. Serve hot, warm, or at room temperature.

Raw Flavor

serves 2

Dried seaweed can be found in Japanese markets as well as in the Asian section of many grocery stores. Cut into thin strips and add to any salad.

ingredients

3 large pieces of seaweed or ¼ cup
purchased seaweed salad
3 to 6 pieces (2 to 3 inches each)
sashimi (tuna, yellowtail, salmon,
or your favorite)
2 tablespoons ginger
1 lemon wedge
2 tablespoons soy sauce

cooking instructions

Place seaweed on a salad plate and top with pieces of sashimi. Serve with ginger and lemon wedge. Place soy sauce in a small cup ramekin for dipping. Hey presto! Sushi heaven...

.

Steamed Vegetables

serves 2

Antioxidant-rich vegetables, walnuts and dried fruit placed on a fluffy bed of leafy rainbow chard. What a colorful and healthy treat!

ingredients

1 medium yellow summer squash, cut into 2-inch pieces

1 medium zucchini, cut into 2-inch pieces

2 large carrots, scrubbed and cut into 2-inch pieces

3 stalks rainbow chard, coarsely chopped if desired

2 tablespoons golden raisins

2 tablespoons brown raisins

1 tablespoon currants

¼ cup walnuts, finely chopped

cooking instructions

Place yellow squash, zucchini, and carrots in a steamer basket over 1 inch of boiling water. Cover and steam over low heat until vegetables are tender, about 3 minutes.

Divide chard between 2 salad plates. Place steamed vegetables over. Sprinkle with raisins, currants, and walnuts.

Green Dream

serves 2

ingredients

2 cups broccoli florets
4 large spears white or green
asparagus
8 green bean pods
2 teaspoons extra virgin olive oil
6 medium shiitake mushrooms,
sliced
3 cloves of garlic, crushed

Juice from 2 lemons
1 bunch kale, coarsely chopped
2 large red tomatoes, coarsely
chopped
Ground black pepper, to taste

cooking instructions

Place broccoli, asparagus and green beans in a steamer basket over 1 inch simmering water. Cover and steam over low heat until vegetables are tender, about 5 minutes.

Heat olive oil in a large sauté pan over medium-high heat. Add mushrooms and sauté until golden brown, about 3 minutes. Add garlic, lemon juice and kale, and cook, stirring frequently until kale has wilted, about 2 minutes.

Divide mushroom mixture between 2 plates. Place steamed vegetables and tomatoes over. Season with pepper and serving.

Side of Squash

serves 2

You can use an acorn squash in place of the yam if you prefer.

ingredients

1 yam, sweet potato, or acorn squash
¼ cup pistachios, coarsely chopped
¼ cup golden raisins, optional
1 tablespoon honey, or to taste

cooking instructions

Preheat oven to 350°F. Pierce yam or squash with a knife to allow steam to escape. Wrap in aluminum foil and bake until center is soft, about 45 minutes. Cut in half horizontally. Add pistachios and raisins over top of cut side. Drizzle with honey and serve.

Lime Chutney

serves 10

This chutney is so delicious on my Gently Curried Lamb (see page 105)!

ingredients

6 limes, quartered
½ medium yellow onion, peeled and quartered
2 hot green chile peppers, stems removed
2 teaspoons chopped fresh ginger
⅓ cup golden raisins
3 green cardamom seeds removed from pods

1 teaspoon black coriander seeds
1 teaspoon mustard seeds
1 teaspoon black peppercorns
2 dried red chile peppers
⅓ cup apple cider vinegar
½ pound brown sugar
1 tablespoon coarse salt

cooking instructions

Place all but 8 of the lime quarters in the bowl of a food processor. Squeeze the juice from remaining lime quarters into the food processor, discarding peel. Add green chile peppers, ginger, and raisins and pulse until finely chopped. Place mixture in a nonmetallic bowl and set aside.

Place cardamom seeds, coriander seeds, mustard seeds, peppercorns, and red chiles in a medium skillet over medium heat and toast, stirring constantly, about 3 minutes. Place on a plate to cool for 5 minutes. Add to a spice grinder or the bowl of a food processor and finely grind. Add ground spice-chile mixture to lime mixture. Add vinegar and sugar and stir well to combine. Cover and let steep at room temperature for two days.

On the third day, pour mixture into an enameled pot (no stainless steel!), add salt, and bring to a boil slowly. Simmer, uncovered, for 30 minutes. Pour into clean, dry glass jars (make sure the jars are completely dry to prevent any mold from forming). Close jars with a tight-fitting lid and store in a cool place, preferably in the refrigerator. The chutney should rest for 2 weeks before opening. Once opened, leftover chutney should always remain refrigerated after use.

Leftover chutney is delicious and with a poached egg and wheat toast for a late breakfast.

Crab Mousse on Hearts of Palm

serves 3 to 4

Luscious whipped crabmeat mousse on top of hearts of palm with an antioxidant-rich pomegranate glaze.

ingredients

Pomegranate glaze:
2 cups pomegranate juice
1 teaspoon granulated sugar
¼ tablespoon salt
1½ tablespoons butter
or butter substitute
3 tablespoons finely chopped
shallots
¼ cup red wine
1 teaspoon lemon juice

Crabmeat mousse:
1 cup boiling water
1 envelope unflavored gelatin
2 cups cooked crabmeat
1 stalk celery, chopped
½ teaspoon salt
1½ tablespoons prepared
horseradish
1½ tablespoons chopped scallions
½ cup nonfat mayonnaise or plain
nonfat yogurt
1 cup heavy cream

cooking instructions

8 pieces hearts of palm, cut in half lengthwise

Seeds from ½ pomegranate (see page 80 for directions on removing seeds)

To make the pomegranate glaze: Place pomegranate juice, sugar, salt, butter, shallots, red wine, and lemon juice in a medium saucepan over medium-high heat. Bring to a boil, reduce heat slightly and let cook, stirring frequently, until glaze is thick enough to coat the back of a spoon, 20 to 30 minutes.

To make the mousse: Place boiling water in a medium bowl and sprinkle gelatin over the top. Stir to dissolve. Let sit a few minutes until thickened. Stir in crabmeat, celery, salt, horseradish, scallions, mayonnaise, and cream.

Divide hearts of palm slices among salad plates and spoon crab mousse over. Drizzle with pomegranate glaze, sprinkle with pomegranate seeds, and serve.

Sweet Potato Snack

Sensationally sweet!

serves 2

ingredients

1 large or two small sweet potatoes
or yams
¼ cup shelled pistachios, coarsely
chopped
2 tablespoons of honey, or to taste

cooking instructions

Preheat oven to 350°F. Pierce sweet potato with a knife and wrap in
aluminum foil. Place on a baking sheet and bake until soft, about 40
minutes. Unwrap and cut in half. Place on a plate and mash slightly
with a fork. Sprinkle with pistachios and drizzle with honey.

Antioxidant Trail Mix

serves 6 to 8

ingredients

2 plain rice cakes, crumbled
8 dried apricots, chopped
1 cup golden raisins
1 cup brown raisins
1 cup raw whole almonds
½ cup walnuts

½ cup sunflower seeds
1 cup goji berries
1½ cups raw chocolate chips or cocoa nibs
1 cup popcorn

cooking instructions

Place all ingredients in a large party bowl (or in individual plastic bags for a great snack while hiking!) and stir to combine.

Follow this great recipe or personalize by purchasing your favorite mixed nuts and simply adding chocolate chunks and your favorite dried fruit! This makes a fun party snack, or place trail mix in individual, serving-size bags for midday snacks or when you're on the go!

Tofu Temptation

serves 2 to 3

ingredients

Juice from 1 lemon
2 tablespoons extra virgin
olive oil
One 7-ounce package silken
organic tofu, cut into bite-size
pieces
1 cup red and green seedless
grapes, cut in half
1 large red beet, peeled and thinly
sliced

1 medium carrot, peeled and
julienned
2 tablespoons pickled ginger
sliced or 2 teaspoons grated fresh
ginger
¼ cup walnut halves
4 cups granola

cooking instructions

Whisk together lemon juice and olive oil in a small bowl. Set aside.

Combine remaining ingredients in a large bowl. Add dressing and toss gently to combine. Serve Tofu Temptation in salad bowls and "give in to temptation"!

Pears and Peppers

serves 2

A wonderful snack from
your market, to your bowl,
for your body and soul!

ingredients

1 cup extra virgin olive oil
Juice from 1 lemon
1 red pear, chopped
1 green pear, chopped
1 yellow pear, chopped
1 medium red onion, chopped

1 red bell pepper, sliced
1 yellow bell pepper, sliced
1 teaspoon chopped cilantro
1 teaspoon fresh rosemary

cooking instructions

Whisk together olive oil and lemon juice in a small bowl until the
mixture has completely emulsified.

Place remaining ingredients in a large bowl and toss with dressing.
Serve immediately.

Sweet Honeydew Prosciutto Dish

serves 4 to 6

ingredients

½ cantaloupe, separated from rind
and sliced into 3" long sticks
6 ounces prosciutto, thinly sliced
½ honeydew melon, cut into cubes
⅓ cup dried cranberries

This tasty dish makes a sweet appetizer for your loved ones or it can be a welcomed addition to a pool party buffet. The sweetness of the melons is a nice contrast to the saltiness of the prosciutto.

cooking instructions

Arrange strips of cantaloupe carefully around the edge of a serving platter. Roll prosciutto loosely and place in a row inside the row of cantaloupe. Place honeydew in the center of the platter. Sprinkle dried cranberries over honeydew. Serve with toothpicks.

The Gold of the Incas

serves 4

Quinoa, a powerful antioxidant, is widely known as "the gold of the Incas". Enjoy this antioxidant-infused delightful dish of grains. Spreading the pumpkin seeds on a baking sheet and toasting them in the oven for a few minutes brings out the flavor and crunch of these nutrient-packed little gems.

ingredients

4 cups low sodium chicken broth
1 cup medium grain brown rice
1 cup quinoa, rinsed and any residue removed
1 tablespoon olive oil
4 shallots, chopped
½ medium yellow onion, chopped

4 garlic cloves
8 ounces cremini or porcini mushrooms, thickly sliced
2 scallions, finely sliced
¼ cup chopped cilantro
12 spears white asparagus
¼ cup raw pumpkin seeds, toasted

cooking instructions

Bring 2 cups chicken broth to a boil in a medium saucepan over high heat. Stir in brown rice, cover, reduce heat to very low, and cook for 45 minutes.

Bring remaining 2 cups chicken broth to a boil in another medium saucepan over high heat. Stir in quinoa, reduce heat, and simmer until tender, about 15 minutes.

Heat olive oil in a skillet over medium-high heat. Add shallots, onions, and garlic, and sauté until lightly golden, about 5 minutes. Add all the mushrooms and cook until golden. Stir in scallions and cilantro. Remove from heat and cover to keep warm.

Place asparagus in a steamer basket over 1 inch of simmering water. Cover and steam until cooked through, about 2 minutes.

To serve, stir together quinoa and brown rice and divide among 4 plates. Add sautéed vegetables and asparagus. Garnish with a scattering of nutritious pumpkin seeds. Serve this warm dish of grains with a tall glass of chilled ice water.

Desserts

Frozen Grape Treat

serves 1

ingredients

2 cups grapes, your favorite kind
1 mint teabag

Use whatever grapes you like for this sweet treat. Concord grapes are my favorite, but black, red, Muscat, globe, and flame grapes are all delicious, too. Pop them in the freezer before you go to bed and overnight you'll have created a great, healthy snack. Enjoy with a cup of mint tea to create a balance between the hot and cold temperatures to awaken your senses. These will last for weeks if placed in an airtight container after freezing, so make extra!

cooking instructions

Rinse grapes and place in a bowl. Place bowl in the freezer for 2 hours or longer. Serve with a steaming hot cup of mint tea.

Gorgeous Grapes

serves 2

ingredients

1½ tablespoons butter
3 tablespoons packed golden brown
sugar
2 red pears, peeled and chopped
Seeds from 1 pomegranate
(see page 80 for removing seeds)
3 cups mixed grapes
(Concord, red seedless, and green)
1 cup walnuts

cooking instructions

Melt butter and brown sugar in the skillet over medium heat. Add pears
and bring mixture to a simmer. Cook, stirring occasionally, until pears
are golden and tender, about 8 minutes. Remove from heat and let cool
to room temperature.

Place pears in a bowl and toss with all the remaining ingredients. Serve
immediately in salad bowls.

Lemon Love

serves 4

Sorbet is a wonderful palate cleanser between courses and after a meal. The meringue cookies are a crisp compliment to the creaminess of the sorbet. Enjoy with a glass of freshly squeezed lemonade. Lemon has many textures to love!

ingredients

3 large egg whites
¼ teaspoon cream of tarter
½ teaspoon vanilla extract
1 cup granulated sugar, plus more to taste for lemonade
Juice from 8 lemons
⅓ cup peanuts

1 tablespoon peanut oil
4 tablespoons turbinado sugar
1 quart lemon sorbet
4 sprigs mint

cooking instructions

Preheat oven to 275°F. Cover a baking sheet with parchment paper and set aside.

Place egg whites in a medium bowl and beat until foamy using an electric mixer. Add cream of tartar and vanilla, and continue beating until egg whites hold soft peaks. Gradually add granulated sugar while beating. Continue to beat the mixture until egg whites are glossy and hold stiff peaks.

Scoop meringue into a zip lock bag and press out any excess air. Cut off a small corner of the bag and squeeze small dollops of meringue onto prepared baking sheet. Bake for 40 minutes until cookies are firm with brown tips.

Combine lemon juice and granulated sugar in a large pitcher. Add purified water and throw in a couple of ice cubes to cool your lemonade.

Increase oven to 325°F. Spray a shallow baking sheet with nonstick cooking spray and set aside.

Toss peanuts with peanut oil and turbinado sugar to coat. Spread on prepared baking sheet and cook until lightly browned, about 6 minutes. Let cool before coarsely chopping or crushing.

Place scoops of sorbet in dessert bowls. Sprinkle with peanuts and garnish with mint sprigs. Serve with lemon meringue cookies.

Seductive Sorbet

serves 2

ingredients

6 ounces prepared
coconut sorbet
3 tablespoons fresh
grated coconut
½ teaspoon cocoa powder
1 mint sprig

This dessert is perfect to share. Make one large serving and serve with two spoons. Many stores sell chunks of fresh coconut meat. If you want to crack your own, place a heavy-duty screwdriver into one of the "eyes" of the coconut and hit with a hammer to drive screwdriver into the coconut, thus cracking the shell. Remove brown membrane with a vegetable peeler. Coconut will keep if refrigerated in an airtight container for up to a week, or frozen for up to 3 months.

Featured in
*L.A. Cooking
Examiner*

cooking instructions

Scoop coconut sorbet into a bowl and sprinkle with coconut. Dust top of sorbet with cocoa powder and garnish with mint sprig.

Whipped Chocolate

serves 2

ingredients

½ container of nonfat whipped
topping
2 containers of nonfat chocolate
pudding
¼ cup dark chocolate chips or organic cocoa nibs
2 large strawberries

cooking instructions

Place whipped topping and pudding in a large bowl and fold together
until mixture is wonderfully fluffy and mousselike. Stir in chocolate
chips. Spoon into 2 glass bowls and garnish each serving with a
strawberry. Simply sweet decadence!

Beverages

Tea Time

serves 2

ingredients

2 green teabags
2 brown or sugar cubes or white
sugar cubes
4 prunes
4 dates
2 figs

¼ cup whole raw almonds
¼ cup raspberries
1 honeycomb or 2 tablespoons
organic honey

cooking instructions

Place 2 to 3 cups of boiling water in a small teapot and add teabags. Let steep for 7 minutes then remove teabags and stir in sugar cubes. Serve tea with prunes, dates, figs, raspberries, almonds, and honeycomb.

Fireplace Moments

serves 2

Serve this hot chocolate with your favorite dark chocolate bar or with dark chocolate truffles. If you really want something inspiring, try a chunk of raw chocolate and infuse it yourself with powerful antioxidants!

ingredients

2 packets dark hot-chocolate mix
½ cup mixed nuts
(almonds, walnuts, macadamia nuts, and pistachios)
1 bar dark chocolate
(approx. 1½ ounces), broken

cooking instructions

Prepare hot chocolate according to package directions. Serve with nuts and chocolate pieces.

Antioxidant "High Juice"

serves 4

ingredients

1 cucumber, washed and unpeeled
8 carrots, washed and unpeeled
4 stalks celery, washed, with leaves
and white bottom portion cut off
Two 1-inch pieces ginger,
unpeeled
1 red beet, scrubbed,
with stems cut off

2 Pink Lady apples
(or any sweet apples you like)
1 bunch chard
3 blood oranges, peeled
2 nectarines, pits removed
1 cup pomegranate seeds
(see page 80 for removing seeds)

cooking instructions

To make the Skin Cleanser High Juice: Add cucumber, 4 carrots, and celery stalks to a juicer and juice to desired consistency.

To make the Liver Cleanser High Juice: Add 1 piece ginger, 4 carrots, red beet to a juicer and juice to desired consistency.

To make the Digestive Cleanser High Juice: Add apples, remaining 1 piece ginger, and chard to a juicer and juice to desired consistency.

To make the Vitamin C Booster and Toxin Cleanser High Juice: Add blood oranges, nectarines, and most of the pomegranate seeds to a juicer and juice to desired consistency. Sprinkle remaining pomegranate seeds into your drink for a textural surprise for your senses.

Invite your dearest friends over for a vegetable juice feast, transforming "high tea" into "high juice". Your body will thank you for the natural high. Serve with your favorite whole wheat crackers and pieces of the vegetables not used to juice. The Greeks associated apples with the healing god Apollo, so sustain your health with this eclectic blend of nature's source of love and health.

Be sure not to peel the carrots and cucumbers as the skin provides most of the nutrients, such as vitamin A, which is found in carrots and is great for eye health.

A Toast to Chocolate

serves 6

ingredients

1 pint of nonfat vanilla ice cream
6 teaspoons raw unsweetened
cocoa powder
Six 12-ounce cans or bottles
Coca-Cola Classic
(or your favorite dark soda)

This is a fun version of the classic root beer float. Raw, dark cocoa powder is a powerful antioxidant. Coca-Cola Classic is a widely known home remedy to soothe one's stomach. So, indulge in the delightful antioxidant power of chocolate with this new take on an old classic. Invite old friends over on a summer night, talk under the stars, and make a toast to embracing change with this new midsummer night's dream!

cooking instructions

Place two small scoops of vanilla ice cream into 6 tall drink glasses. Sprinkle cocoa powder over the ice cream. Slowly pour Coca-Cola into each glass, being careful not to let it overflow. Leave the can or bottle with your guest, so they can add more as the ice-cream vanishes . . . it tends to do that quite quickly!

Watermelon "Martini" Slushy

serves 6

ingredients

6 cups watermelon, cut into 1-inch
pieces and frozen
Juice from 1 lemon
2 cups lemon- or lime-flavored
seltzer water
2 tablespoons sugar substitute
6 ½-inch watermelon cubes for
garnish
Mint sprigs for garnish

cooking instructions

Place frozen watermelon in a blender. Add lemon juice, seltzer water,
and sugar substitute. Puree until slushy.

Pour into martini glasses and garnish with a mint sprig and a small cube
of watermelon on the edge of glass. The perfect accompaniment to a hot
summer's day—or evening!

Chapter 11

Antioxidant Beauty Bytes

As crucial as it is to nourish the inside of your body with antioxidant-rich recipes for glowing skin, it is equally important to nurture your inner beauty by caring for your body, externally with the Beauty Bytes in this chapter.

These Beauty Bytes will offer helpful tips and secrets for being your most beautiful, authentic self. Indulge your beautiful self, you deserve it!

Silky Milk

Add milk to your bath for smoother skin all over your body. Before there were sophisticated lotions, women of royalty or aristocracy would bathe in milk for the smoothing benefits it had for their oh-so-delicate skin. So treat yourself like a queen, and add a splash of milk to your bath. About 1 cup will do or use two for ultimate luxury!

Spa Water

In a pitcher of ice water, add thinly sliced cucumber. Play your favorite song to set the "spa mood".

Sunny Legs

Finely ground sunflower seeds can be added to shaving cream to exfoliate your legs. Exfoliation removes a layer of dead skin cells, revealing softer legs. While this recipe works wonders for your legs, I do not recommend this for facial exfoliation because the skin on your face is far more delicate.

"Thou shalt prove that beauty is no beauty without love."
—Thomas Campion

Chocolate Choppers

Dark chocolate is an antioxidant, so no need to worry about chocolate as a cause of blemishes on your skin. Raw chocolate is an even greater antioxidant because it is unprocessed. Eric Shapira, a spokesperson for the Academy of General Dentistry, explains that dark chocolate (characterized as chocolate with at least 80 percent cocoa) contains chemicals that fight plaque build-up on teeth. This is great news! Chocolate to improve your smile? A smile is a reflection of inner joy, so show your joy to the people you love and smile at them. Adding several chips of raw chocolate to any blender drink is a great way to improve your skin, while helping to wake you up!

My Antioxidant Trail Mix on page 134 packed with your favorite mixed nuts and raw, dark chocolate hunks, is a great way to enjoy a treat when hiking!

Fancy Fragrant Bath

Pear-scented candles are refreshing. For your next bath, clear your mind and surround yourself with the crisp aroma of burning pear-scented candles. Use this opportunity to meditate and find your center, while deeply breathing in the soothing aroma of the pear-scented candles. Taking in deep breaths of oxygen is a gift to your skin. After your bath, you will dry off feeling refreshed, alive, and peaceful with a beautiful state of mind.

Hydrating Body Scrub

Hydration and moisture retention is essential for smooth, supple skin. Circulation is an important part of fighting the appearance of cellulite and we can use this hydrating body scrub to help with both of these issues at once! Cocoa powder and coffee grounds improve circulation, especially when rubbed over legs and thighs. They also work as an exfoliant. Almond oil is high in vitamin E, which helps your skin retain its moisture, and it is a powerful antioxidant. Shea butter is an extremely hydrating cream-like substance, and it is also has anti-inflammatory properties—perfect for a heavenly body scrub that smells divine!

Ingredients:
3 tablespoons almond oil
1 teaspoon coffee grounds
1 teaspoon cocoa powder
1 tablespoon shea butter

Mix all ingredients together in a small bowl. Apply to clean skin in the shower, while rubbing in a circular motion. Try to stay out of the shower stream while rubbing in this very hydrating, natural body scrub. Rinse thoroughly and you will have smooth, supple skin.

Citrus Circulation

Use the rind of an orange and rub the outer textured side of the orange peel against your thighs and buttocks to increase circulation. I recommend taking a shower promptly afterward, not only to remove any residue but also because the steam and heat of the shower will continue to increase circulation. Proper circulation can help reduce the appearance of unsightly veins on the legs. Fight fire with fire! Use orange peel to tackle the bumpy, orange-peel appearance we get from from cellulite.

Restful Rosemary

Create your own rosemary incense. Add a teaspoon of rosemary spice to a small dish of aromatic oil, and place a lighted candle a few inches underneath it. The flames will capture the soothing aroma of the rosemary. You can enjoy this as a centerpiece with dinner, infusing your body with a rosemary experience, touching it, seeing it, tasting it, and smelling it.

Beaming Berry

Berries have powerful antioxidant and anti-inflammatory abilities. Let a berry and wine sauce replace a mayonnaise or tartar sauce, which can clog your pores. Indulge in my Antioxidant Berry Glaze (see page 83), drizzled over my Pretty Poached Salmon on page 83. Your skin will thank you with a beaming, glowing complexion. The berry glaze is made by pureeing blackberries, raspberries, and honey in a blender or small food processor until nearly smooth.

Delicate Décolleté

As softening as honey is for the hands and for the face, it is also good for soothing your neck's dry skin. The skin on our neck is more delicate and thinner than the skin on the rest of our body, so it needs special attention. Mix 2 tablespoons honey with 2 tablespoons milk. A thin layer of honey smoothed over your entire neck and chest area in an upward motion is just what nature ordered. Do not forget your décolleté. Take a bubble bath and wash away the honeyed neck mask after ten minutes.

Superior Shaving

Olive oil makes a wonderfully skin-softening shaving cream. The silky sensation of this homemade shaving cream is also hydrating, so rub an extra amount over your knees and the heels on your feet.

Sea Salt Scrub

Coarse sea salt is an exfoliator, removing dead skin cells, while almond oil helps the skin retain moisture. Mix 1 cup of coarse sea salt with enough almond oil to create a grainy mixture. Massage mixture onto your legs for a smoother shave. This has the interesting skin health benefit of simultaneously exfoliating and moisturizing.

Honeyed Hands

"Honeyed hands" may sound finger-licking good, but it is finger-smoothing good too. Find two clean socks that you do not mind discarding after use. Use a paintbrush or a synthetic fiber makeup brush and get ready to become a living work of art. Dip the brush into a jar of raw honey and generously paint a layer of honey, about ¼ inch-thick, onto one hand and then cover with one of the socks. Then, with your honey-mitten hand, do the same for your other hand. Leave on for thirty minutes and then rinse off thoroughly. Your hands are another revealer of age, so smooth out and soften your hands and reverse the clock.

"The fairest hand I ever touched: O beauty, till now I never know thee."
—William Shakespeare

Fabulous Feet

Macadamia nut oil preserves youth. Aside from the virtue of consuming this oil internally, there is also value in using macadamia nut oil and other oils externally on the skin. No other part of your skin is subject to more abuse than your feet. Your poor, dry, calloused feet are aching for some attention and soothing relief. Love your feet by creating a footbath of warm water, ¼ cup of natural macadamia nut oil, and squeeze in some lemon juice as well. Remember that lemon is antibacterial, which could help prevent skin irritation or fungal problems. The skin on the bottom of your feet desires to be soft and beautiful too!

Cinnamon Foot Indulgence

Cinnamon sticks, or quills, can be dried and ground into powder to create the tasty, aromatic spice of cinnamon. There are many noted health benefits of cinnamon, specifically in helping to ease digestion or nausea. Cinnamon is also known to ease the painful cramps associated with a woman's menstrual cycle. So if you are experiencing cramps at "that time of the month", treat yourself to a relaxing, calming, Cinnamon Foot Indulgence. Breathe in the aroma of the cinnamon and enjoy your foot-bathing experience. Give your heels reprieve from pounding the pavement, and nurture your delicate feet.

Cinnamon spice (ground powder) can be purchased at your local market, or found in your pantry.

Ingredients:
Juice from 5 organic lemons
(remove seeds from juice using a fork)
Olive oil, 1 tablespoon
¼ cup whole milk
½ cup water

Mix all ingredients together and place in your tub or other foot-sized bucket. Slather all over your heels (perfect for dry, cracked skin), the balls of your feet, and those "little piggies!" Allow feet to soak in the Cinnamon Foot Indulgence bath for 15 -20 minutes. Rinse with warm water, or just jump into the tub and enjoy the healing aroma of the cinnamon.

Citrus Clean

The next time you are washing your face with soap, add a squeeze of natural lemon juice. Lemon is a natural antibacterial agent and will leave your skin ultra cleansed. Lemon also acts as a great skin toner, leaving your beautifully cleansed skin feeling tightened too!

Brightening Face Mask

Vitamin C is a potent antioxidant, which helps fight cellular damage and improve the skin's elasticity. It is wonderful for preventing wrinkles and is known to brighten the complexion. Lime juice has a high amount of vitamin C and Alpha Hydroxy Acids (AHA), which are also known to brighten skin. Tumeric powder is a non-drying disinfectant and a good skin clarifying agent. Olive oil is a gentle, natural moisturizer. This mask will reveal your glowing complexion, so say goodbye to dull skin with this all-natural, Brightening Face Mask.

Ingredients:
1½ teaspoons Gram flour
inch Tumeric powder
1 teaspoon olive oil
1 teaspoon whole milk
⅓ teaspoon juice from 1 organic lime

Mix all ingredients together in a small bowl. Apply to a clean face, and leave on until your skin begins to feel tight, approximately 15 minutes. Note that the potency of this mask expires in about a week, as the natural process of oxidation affects the ingredients upon exposure to the air.

Lavender Steam Facial

Over the stove, bring a medium-sized pot of water to a high heat (almost boil). Add a few drops of lavender oil for a calming aroma. Pull your hair back, away from your face, and lean over the pot of Lavender Steam. Hold a towel over your head, covering the pot, to allow the natural steam facial to open your pores. Inhale the lavender aroma with deep, relaxing breaths. After five breaths, your skin will have a wet sheath of sweat. With a cold, damp washcloth, pat your face to seal the pores with the cool temperature of the cloth. This Lavender Steam Facial improves hydration, which is the secret to supple skin.

Pomegranate Pout

The juice of the pomegranate can be painted on your lips with a lip brush to create a beautiful berry lip stain. Wearing an antioxidant lip gloss will also help protect your luscious lips from free radicals in the environment. Fabulously healthy and pretty!

Luscious Lips

The summer heat can be harsh and cause chapped lips or even sun-blisters. Use the rest of the cucumber from the Spa Water Beauty Byte on page 164 to restore moisture to dry lips.

Peel the cucumber and puree it in the blender to extract the juice. Add just 1 tablespoon of honey and 1 tablespoon of plain yogurt, then stir until your homemade lip balm is blended. Apply like lip-gloss and allow it to absorb into your lips.

Tight Toning

Balsamic vinegar is tantalizing to the taste buds and also acts as a toner when applied to the skin. Apple cider vinegar is ideal to use as a toning astringent to tighten and tone the skin. This is not only beneficial for the face, but for the rest of your body too. In fact, if you use powdered facial masks that require water to create a paste, substitute apple cider vinegar in place of water to greatly improve results.

Honey Moisturizing

Honey is a natural moisturizer for the skin. A thin layer of honey, left on the face for fifteen to twenty minutes, is a wonderful moisturizing mask. Add 1 cup honey with 1 cup brown sugar for an exfoliating body scrub in the shower. Delicious!

Honey Skin Clearing Mask

Honey is a natural antibacterial agent, and this mask is your step towards a clear complexion! Carrots are rich in vitamin A, and the nutrients are in the skins, so no need to peel the carrots in this Beauty Byte...just wash well!

Bring a pot of hot water to a boil. Throw in six carrots, cut into chunks with the skins on. Boil until the carrots are soft, approximately 15 minutes. Mash them in a bowl. Add 6 tablespoons of organic honey and 4 drops of lavender oil. Mix until you have a smooth orange paste. Place in the refrigerator for 10 minutes to let cool. Remove from the refrigerator and apply to your face, avoiding the eyes. It is a good idea to use a tongue depressor for application to avoid depositing the oil and germs from your fingertips onto your face. Leave on for 10 minutes and rinse with cool water to seal the pores.

NOTE: If you have a pimple, dab some Neosporin ointment on the blemish. It is antibacterial and will help your pimple to heal faster. If you do not have any Neosporin in your medicine cabinet, you can use some toothpaste, which will help dry out the blemish.

Green Tea Extract Cream

All ingredients for this Green Tea Extract Cream can be purchased at your local health food store. Green tea extract is known to suppress inflammation, while shea butter and peppermint oil are both known to stimulate cell generation. This potent antioxidant Beauty Byte is fabulous for improving Rosacea and is so simple to whip up at home!

Simply mix the green tea extract, shea butter, and peppermint oil until it becomes creamy. Apply this cream nightly to areas of your face affected by Rosacea.

NOTE: Rosacea can often be drastically improved by avoiding the ingestion of spicy foods, which tend to trigger the symptoms of this skin woe. However, Green Tea is widely known as a natural healing agent and drinking green tea can also help improve Rosacea.

Perfect Pores

If your facialist is out of town, fear not! Boil water in a pot over the stove and allow the steam to rise to your face. The heat and the moisture will open your skin's pores and release oxidants and toxins. When you feel as though your face has a sheath of wetness covering it, immediately cleanse with cool water to rinse away the toxins you have sweated out and seal your pores. This is a cleansing, natural way to release your skin of undesirable toxins. It's your at-home facial.

Luxury Clay

Bentonite clay absorbs toxins from the skin and exfoliates, thus improving skin circulation. Apple cider vinegar has natural antibacterial properties and is known to improve acne. Mix together 1/2 tablespoon of Bentonite clay with 1 tablespoon of apple cider vinegar. Stir until mask becomes a creamy paste. Apply to face, avoiding eye area. Leave clay mask on for 10 minutes and rinse with cold water to seal the pores.

Rosy Complexion

Green tea is an anti-inflammatory with healing properties. Rose water is derived from the beauty of the rose. It aids with circulation and digestion, and has value as a toning astringent. Steep green tea and add to rose water in a 1:1 ratio. Place in a mister and use as an astringent on a clean face, before applying moisturizer. It smells divine.

Sun Soothing

After a day at the beach, enjoying the sun's warm rays (with sunscreen, of course!) squeeze a handful of red seedless grapes into a small bowl. Use a fork to smash the grapes. Squeeze the juice out and splash the "antioxidant juice" onto your face. It will soothe your skin from your recent sun exposure. Always follow your sun-grape beauty routine by cleansing your face afterwards.

Apple Cider Acne Cream

Apple cider vinegar, rich in vitamin A, is essential for improving acne. In fact, a lack of vitamin A has been known to worsen the appearance of acne. Apple cider vinegar is a natural product, and can typically be found in your local market. Tomatoes have more nutritional value once they have been cooked, so using a tomato paste has more benefits than a raw tomato.

Mix together ¼ cup low-sodium tomato paste, 1 teaspoon olive oil, and apple cider vinegar until you have a smooth paste. Use as a neck and facial mask to alleviate acne. Leave on for 15 minutes and then gently rinse off with warm water. Finally, splash some cold water on your face to immediately close your pores.

NOTE: Go ahead and drink some of the apple cider vinegar, as well. It is a great detoxifier and has a natural effect of weight loss and removing toxins from your body.

Avocado Smoothing Facial

Avocados can replenish moisture to the skin. An avocado mask can improve very dry skin, smoothing your skin to its natural supple state. Smash half of one avocado until whipped, and apply a thin layer of this skin softening mixture to your face, avoiding the eye area. Rinse with warm water, and then a splash of cold water, to close the pores.

Bright Persimmon Peels

Sunspots and other mild discolorations call for a brightening of your complexion. Beta-carotene and vitamin C are vital for maintaining a bright complexion. Certain foods are known for improving skin discolorations, yet there is a special fruit that brightens your complexion internally and topically! This delicious, special fruit is the persimmon. I grew up with a huge persimmon tree in my backyard and the antioxidant treat was sweet and given to me as dessert! My fondness for persimmons has expanded as I came to know the depths of its nutritional value for brightening one's complexion.

Find a ripe organic persimmon at your local market. Peel the persimmon, laying the fresh peel on a paper towel. Slice the remaining fruit and enjoy as a raw food treat, which internally helps to brighten one's complexion.

This generous fruit also has many benefits applied topically. On a cleansed face, place the fresh persimmon peels on your skin, focusing on the areas of discoloration. Lay down and relax for 15 minutes while the persimmon peels work their magic! Rinse your face with cool water to close the pores. If there are some persimmon peels that you did not use on your skin, then feel free to eat them! Enjoy. It's a bright, new day!

Lemonade out of Lemons

Lemons are naturally antibacterial and act as a natural astringent. For oily skin, the most important thing is to avoid removing too much oil, wherein your body overcompensates and actually produces more oil. I recommend a gentle, delicate approach to healing oily skin, naturally.

Simply mix 1 teaspoon of water with 1 teaspoon of the juice of one organic lemon. Be sure to pick out the lemon's seeds from the teaspoon—this is not an exfoliation! Gently splash the mixture onto your clean face and allow it to absorb into your skin. Rinse off with cool water to close the pores. There's nothing bitter about this lemon Beauty Byte!

Toning Tomato

Lycopene, a powerful antioxidant in tomatoes, becomes more bioavailable to our bodies when heated or cooked, so our bodies can absorb more of this wonderful antioxidant. So, using a tomato paste has more benefits than using a raw tomato. Mix together ¼ cup of low-sodium tomato paste, 1 teaspoon of olive oil, and 4 teaspoons of apple cider vinegar until you have a smooth paste. Use it as a neck and facial mask. Leave the mask on for 15 minutes and then gently rinse with warm water. Finally, splash some cold water on your face to close your pores.

Apple Cider Mist

Fill up a mister or spray bottle with a 1:1 ratio of apple cider vinegar to purified water. Mist your face after your regular cleansing routine. It will act as a topical astringent toner.

Go ahead and drink some of the apple cider vinegar, as well. It is detoxifying and has a natural effect of weight loss and is very effective at removing toxins from your body.

Tantalizing Tea

A chilled, wet teabag, placed over the skin directly under the eye can reduce under-eye puffiness. For more sensitive skin, the herbs in chamomile tea soothe the face. Echinacea is a natural antibiotic and anti-inflammatory herbal plant, and teas with echinacea in them are excellent for reducing puffiness under the eyes. You can also use spinach leaves to reduce eye inflammations, placing the leaves in a small teabag or in a slightly wetted napkin, and then over your eyes. Goodbye puffy eyes!

Placing teabags over your closed eyes can do much more than just de-puff. The teabag actually draws toxins away from your eyes. So, if your eyes are irritated from an eyelash or mascara, sooth your eyes and your soul with a relaxing tea detox.

Grateful Grapes

Another way to diminish under-eye puffiness is to place a frozen grape under each eye. Frozen grapes won't melt as quickly as ice cubes and they are also the perfect size to cover the delicate, fine skin underneath your eye. You can also place frozen grapes inside a sleeping mask so they stay in place. Enjoy a warm bath while your eyes de-puff! No sour grapes here!

Bright Eyes

Featured in Discovery Channel's *Planet Green*

Place 2 small spoons in your refrigerator for several minutes (or even overnight if you'd like to try this Beauty Byte first thing in the morning). Upon awakening to those dark circles under your eyes, gently lay the spoons directly under each eye. Be careful to use minimal pressure as the skin under your eyes is sensitive. You should feel refreshed and "bright-eyed". Lightly dab some cucumber juice underneath the eyes, and begin your beautiful day!

"Pump some iron" into your diet and say goodbye to dark circles. Foods that contain iron, like dark leafy greens such as kale and spinach, can vastly improve your eyes' dark secret!

Black Olive Eye Treatment

Black olives are a great natural source of vitamin E, and a wonderful topical source for a variety of skin ailments including scars, discolorations, and fine lines. Black olives actually contain an anti-bacterial antioxidant. Ingesting or externally applying antioxidant remedies promotes the reparation of damaged skin cells.

Pour some extra virgin olive oil into a small bowl. Finely slice the black olives and saturate them by placing them in the bowl to absorb the olive oil. Gently remove the olive slices and place around the outer optical bone so that you have a half-moon of olives resting on each eye, where most fine lines have a tendency to develop. Draw a bath and place a dry wash cloth over your eyes to hold the black olives in place. Keep eyes closed. After 15 minutes, remove olives and gently massage the remaining olive oil into your skin around the outer eye area.

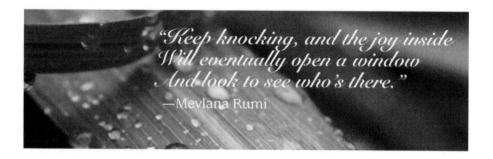

"Keep knocking, and the joy inside
Will eventually open a window
And look to see who's there."
—Mevlana Rumi

Angelic Eyes

If the eyes are the windows into our souls, then we should care for them like precious gems. Broccoli is rich in antioxidants, specifically phytochemical arotenoid antioxidants known as lutein and zeaxanthin. "Lutien/zeaxanthin serves to protect the eyes from the free-radical damage done to the eyes by ultraviolet light." Enjoy some broccoli, open your eyes, and let others see into your joyous, beautiful soul.

Luscious Locks

Naturally squeezed grapefruit juice added to extra virgin olive oil can act as a hair-moisturizing and cleansing mask. The oil reinvigorates a dry scalp, and seals split ends. Meanwhile, the juice of the grapefruit adds a pleasant aroma, and functions as a cleansing agent to purify your luscious locks. Squeeze one whole pink grapefruit in a small bowl and remove the seeds. Add two tablespoons of extra virgin olive oil and distribute evenly over hair and scalp, leaving in for a few minutes. Shampoo as usual.

Healthy Hair

Take ⅓ cup of extra virgin olive oil and heat it in the microwave for 25 seconds until warm. Before shampooing your hair, work the oil throughout your scalp and hair. There are various hot oil treatments available at drugstores and now, you can make your own in your kitchen.

Lustrous Locks

For lustrous locks of hair, break open an organic egg and beat well. Smooth the egg into the ends of your dry hair. Massage into hair for five minutes to seal split-ends and moisturize strands of hair. Follow with a thorough shampoo and deep conditioning. Nothing compliments a glowing complexion like healthy, shiny hair.

Soothing Honey Steam Treatment

Featured on YoungHollywood.com

Gym-goers, listen up! After an intense work-out, the steam room becomes an opportunity to release toxins through your pores for a glowing complexion. Honey is a natural moisturizer and has antibacterial properties. It is the perfect cleansing and hydrating mask. Splash your face with warm water and gently coat your face with honey, avoiding the eye-area. Step into the steam room for a few minutes and rinse your face with cool water to seal the pores.

You can even apply honey to your hair while steaming as a natural deep conditioning treatment. Wash your hair before entering the steam room, and towel dry. Apply honey as a hair mask to the ends of your damp hair, avoiding the "crown" of your head. Put it in a clip and enjoy your steam. Nature's honey will give your skin an extra glow, and your hair will shine! Simple and all-natural.

Calming Green

Like all antioxidants, spinach leaves are an anti-inflammatory. Reducing inflammation is a pivotal part of achieving clear, glowing skin. Cooking with more leafy greens, such as spinach, is a brilliant way to cook for beauty!

Glorious Grains

Whole grains, like brown rice, strengthen the intestines. This makes it easier for your body to eliminate harmful toxins. Your body eliminates toxins in different ways—one of which is through the skin. This may be evident as a blemish or a cystic pimple. Your diet is a crucial part of keeping your skin beautiful and clear. Cook with whole grains for beauty.

Fabulous Fiber

Oat bread is high in fiber. "Studies show that fiber reduces cholesterol absorption and increases insulin sensitivity," explains Denis Lairon, Ph.D. The reduction of cholesterol absorption is a major health benefit for so many Americans whose diet consists mainly of fast food and other high caloric meals. *Cooking Well: Beautiful Skin* is a way to eat healthy for your body, mind, and spirit. Bon Appetit!

Generous Ginger

Ginger is often served with sushi because it has antibacterial qualities. Ginger also prevents nausea. "Ginger might suppress serotonin, which helps to trigger nausea," explains Nathorn Chaiyakunapruk, Ph.D. It is anti-inflammatory and known to soothe cramps associated with menstrual cycles. Ginger offers so many health benefits. Thank you ginger!

Healing Honey

Organic honeycomb is mother nature's moisturizer and can be found at your local farmer's market. It also has medical, healing qualities for your throat, if ingested, as it is an anti-inflammatory substance. Thank you buzzy bees!

Nuts and Nature

Nuts are a major source of vitamin E, which contains great healing properties for scarred skin. Do not worry about the next adventurous mountain biking afternoon. Enjoy yourself and feel free. If you get a scrape, you can count on vitamin E infused foods, like nuts, to lessen the scar. Keep your skin unmarked with Antioxidant Trail Mix on page 134. However, these ingredients alone are not a substitute in any way for medical attention or a doctor's visit to improve the aesthetics of an unsightly scar. Dermatologists and plastic surgeons can offer many creams, which include vitamin E, and other more advanced methods of scar healing.

Miraculous Mint

Mint has beneficial digestive qualities and is quite soothing to your stomach and your nerves. In order to filter toxins properly (so that your body does not need to filter the toxins through the surface of your skin in the form or blemishes or pimples), it is important that your digestive track is functioning well. Eating mint leaves or drinking mint tea is a good way to ensure that your skin does not wind up becoming responsible for filtering your body's toxins in an unbeautiful way.

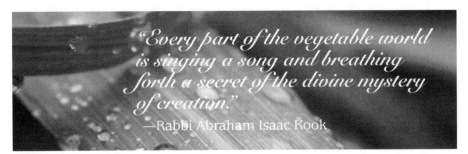

"Every part of the vegetable world is singing a song and breathing forth a secret of the divine mystery of creation."
—Rabbi Abraham Isaac Kook

Lovely Lycopene

Cooking with tomatoes is essentially cooking for beauty. Tomatoes have high levels of the nutrient lycopene. As Steven Pratt and Kathy Matthews write in their book *Superfoods: Fourteen Foods that Will Change Your Life,* "Lycopene is an important part of the antioxidant defense network in the skin, and dietary lycopene by itself in combination with other nutrients can raise the sun protection factor (SPF) of the skin." So, cooking with tomatoes ultimately bathes your skin in sunscreen from the inside out!

Fantastic Figs

Figs are actually a higher source of calcium than oranges. Cooking with figs as an additional ingredient is delicious, but also very good for strengthening bones. Strong bones can improve posture, which is always beautiful. So, stand tall and let your inner strength radiate!

"Beauty is power; a smile its sword."
—Charles Reade

Energetic Egg

Egg whites are rich in protein. "Protein-rich foods replenish cells, and that helps keep blood flowing to the nerve endings inside your teeth." Who knew some egg whites could make you smile so wide?

The protein in egg whites is also great for providing an energy boost.

Long Live Gogi Berries

Tibetan goji berries are the secret to anti-aging! Many Tibetans credit the goji berry for their secret to longevity. The legendary Li Qing Yuen, who is believed to have lived to the age of 252 years (1678–1930), consumed goji berries daily. I believe that with a long life come wisdom and the potential for a deeper understanding of self-love, as well as love for our fellow beings in the universe. As beauty shines from the inside out, we should turn our thoughts to living each day to its fullest and brightest, living with self-love, so our inner beauty can radiate to the world for as long as we walk on it.

Powerful Parsley

Parsley has healing qualities for your mouth, so munching on some after every meal will leave your breath fresh. Confidence and self-worth are part of our goals in *Cooking Well: Beautiful Skin*, and fresh breath can help you achieve the confidence you desire. And what better way to learn about yourself than to spend time with others? Let the beautiful green parsley be the first step toward self-knowledge and confidence. Yes, it's true. There is a connection between a bunch of parsley and self-love. There are connections in all things in life, if we take the time to care about noticing them. So, do not run through life without intention. Stop, and smell the parsley.

Digestive Delight

Cleanse your body and improve absorption of nutrients by adding a tiny dash of cayenne pepper to your next freshly squeezed glass of lemonade, and reap the digestive track benefits. Bye-bye, bloat!

Sensory Sorbet

Sorbet is known to cleanse your palate. So, after you have enjoyed an antioxidant rich recipe, have some Seductive Sorbet (see page 148). This will also improve your breath. There is always room for kisses after dessert!

Youthful Yellow Pepper

One large, yellow bell pepper contains approximately 341mg of calcium. The higher your intake of such nutrients, the slower you will age. A youthful complexion is one of the virtues of beauty, so enjoy your youthful appearance with a side of yellow bell peppers!

Hello Histamines!

Awaken your senses and breathe in deeply when you indulge in Chile Pepper Chicken (page 104), an antioxidant-rich meal. The chile peppers and mustard act as a wake-up shock to the histamines in your nose. Enjoy the invigorating sensation of smell and taste. Hot, hot hot!

"Anyone who keeps the ability to see beauty never grows old."
—Franz Kafka

Glamorous Garlic

Garlic has an impressive array of healing attributes. It actually nurtures the good bacteria in your stomach lining, thereby strengthening your body's immunity to infections. It has antiviral agents, cholesterol reducers, decongestants, anti-inflammatory agents, and even blood pressure reducers. High blood pressure is considered to be more dangerous than high cholesterol. Lower blood pressure is a sign of lower levels of anxiety or stress. This is incredibly important for glowing skin because stress creates breakouts and other unglamorous blemishes. So eat your garlic, and stay glamorous!

Closing Thoughts

Maintain Your Glow

Now that you have reached these last pages, you have likely come to embody a sense of inner sanctity and, consequently, a beautiful and natural external glow. I sincerely hope that the many antioxidant-rich recipes in this book have helped you feel lighter, as though you are walking on air. This sensation of weightlessness has less to do with a tangible weight and more to do with a light-hearted spirit. Your spirit has been awakened by you, and by your choice to turn your attention inward, thereby enabling you to gain a greater perspective of yourself as a whole.

This longing and searching for the knowledge of who you are, completely, is my definition of self-love. The act of valuing yourself, and the quest for self-awareness, brings you to a heightened self-consciousness. This is living meditation—a road map to your truest self.

You will attain beauty with the proper choice of nutrients that will nourish yourself and enhance your mind and body, giving you the energy of vitality, and of beauty. Without our inner identity, we are but empty shells. Outer beauty cannot exist without inner beauty.

There is beauty that deserves to be recognized in your mind, your heart, and your soul. Connect with your authentic, inner self, and the beauty that exists within each part of you will become grand; your consciousness of your beauty will expand in all directions, touching all those around you. You will radiate beauty for others to experience, and realize that you are indeed a far more beautiful person than you may have dreamed you are.

Nurture your beautiful inner self, and your love and spirit will set your face aglow with beauty.

"Though we seem
to be sleeping,
There is an inner
wakefulness
That directs the dream
And that will eventually
startle us back
To the truth of
who we are."
—Mevlana Rumi

"The philosophic spirit
of inquiry may be
traced to brute curiosity,
and that to the habit of
examining all things in
search of food."
—W. Winwood Reade

References

Chapter 2
1. Maslow, Abraham, H., *Toward a Psychology of Being* (New York: Van Nostrand, 1962).

Chapter 5
2. Bowen & Bowen. *"Crystal Refreshing Drinking Water."* Berkley Springs International Water Tasting, 2003.
3. Emoto, Masaru, *The Hidden Messages in Water.* Trans. Thayne, David A. (Beyond Words Publishing: Hillsboro, Oregon, 2004).
4. Squires, Sally. *"The Bottle-Versus-the-Tap Debate."* Los Angeles Times July 17, 2006: p 2.

Chapter 6
5. Siler, Brooke, *The Pilates Body* (New York: Broadway Books, 2000), 16–17.

Chapter 8
6. Cabot, Sandra M.D. *The Liver Cleansing Diet.* Scottsdale, AZ: SCB International, 2008.
7. Bragg, Paul C., N.D., Ph.D., and Patricia Bragg, N.D., Ph.D. Apple Cider Vinegar: Miracle Health System. Santa Barbara: Bragg Health Sciences, 2008.

Chapter 9
8. Royle, David. 2003. *Body Perfect.* http://www.nationalgeographic.com/series/taboo/1851/overview [2003].
9. ibid.
10. Illes, Judith, *Tour Egypt Monthly Online Magazine, Volume 1, No. 1, "Beauty Secrets of Ancient Egypt"*, June 1, 2000.
11. *Maori Goddess of Beauty.* http://www.maori.com/kmst5.htim/ [May 2006].
12. ibid.
13. Burkhart, Brad, *"Birth Worship,"* maori.com/kmstl.htm, 1997

Chapter 10
14. Hopkins, Martha, and Lockridge, Randall, *Intercourses: An Aphrodisiac Cookbook* (Memphis, TN: Terrace Publishing, 1997), 64.

Chapter 11
15. Shapira, Eric, D.D.S. *"Eat for your Teeth."* Women's Health Magazine May 2006: 22.
16. Pratt, Steven M.D., and Kathy Matthews, Super Foods: Fourteen Foods That Will Change Your Life. New York: Harper Collins Publishing, 2004.
17. Carper, Jean, Stop *Aging Now: The Ultimate Plan for Staying Young & Reversing the Aging Process* (New York: Harper Collins Publishers, 1995).
18. Kurz, Susan West, and Monte, Tom, *Awakening Beauty the Dr. Hauschka Way* (New York: Clarkson Potter Publishers, 2006).
19. ibid.
20. Kurz, Susan West, and Monte, Tom, *Awakening Beauty: the Dr. Hauschuka Way* (New York, Clarkson Potter Publishers, 2006).
21. Wolfe, David. *Eating for Beauty.* North Atlantic Books, 2003.
22. Pratt, Steven M.D., and Matthews, Kathy, *Super Foods: Fourteen Foods That Will Change Your Life* (New York: HarperCollins, 2004).
23. ibid.
24. Carper, Jean, *Stop Aging Now: The Ultimate Plan for Staying Young & Reversing the Aging Process* (New York: Harper Collins, 1995).
25. Shapira, Eric, D.D.S. *"Eat for your Teeth."* Women's Health Magazine May 2006: 22.
26. ibid.

27. ibid.
28. Pratt, Steven M.D., and Kathy Matthews, *Super Foods: Fourteen Foods That Will Change Your Life*. New York: Harper Collins Publishing, 2004.
29. ibid.
30. Wolfe, David. *Eating for Beauty*. North Atlantic Books, 2003.
31. Shapira, Eric, D.D.S. *"Eat for your Teeth." Women's Health Magazine* May 2006: 22.
32. www.essentiallivingfoods.com Superfruits: Goji Berries [March, 2006].
33. Pratt, Steven M.D., and Matthews, Kathy, *Super Foods: Fourteen Foods That Will Change Your Life* (New York: HarperCollins, 2004).
34. ibid.
35. Carper, Jean. *Stop Aging Now: The Ultimate Plan for Staying Young & Reversing the Aging Process*. New York: Harper Collins Publishers, Inc., 1995.

Additional Resources

Aihara, Herman. *Acid & Alkaline, Fifth Edition*. Oroville, CA: George Ohsawa Macrobiotic Foundation, 1986.

Apostle, Hippocrates G. and Lloyd P. Gerson. *Aristotle Selected Works, 3rd Edition*. Grinnell, IA: The Peripatetic Press, 1991.

Brotman, Juliano, and Erika Lenkert. *Raw: The Uncook Book: New Vegetarian Food for Life*. New York: Regan Books, 1999.

Burroughs, Stanley. *The Master Cleanse: With Special Needs and Problems*. Reno: Burroughs Books, 1976.

Mindell, Earl, R.Ph., Ph.D. *Herb Bible*. New York: Fireside Publishers, 1992.

Meyerowitz, Steve. *Wheat Grass: Nature's Finest Medicine*. Summertown, TN: Book Publishing Company, 1999.

Phillips, Bill. *Eating for Life*. Golden, CO: High Point Media, 2003.

Turner, Kristina. *The Self-Healing Cookbook: Whole Foods to Balance Body, Mind, & Moods*. Vashon Island, WA: Earthtones Press, 1987.

My Recipes

My Recipes

My Recipes

My Recipes

My Recipes

My Recipes